Risk Analysis in Project Appraisal

Risk Analysis in Project Appraisal:

Assessment of Risk and Return in Capital Investment Decisions

By

Savvakis C. Savvides

Cambridge Scholars Publishing

Risk Analysis in Project Appraisal:
Assessment of Risk and Return in Capital Investment Decisions

By Savvakis C. Savvides

This book first published 2025

Cambridge Scholars Publishing

Lady Stephenson Library, Newcastle upon Tyne, NE6 2PA, UK

British Library Cataloguing in Publication Data
A catalogue record for this book is available from the British Library

ISBN: 978-1-0364-4778-6
ISBN (Ebook): 978-1-0364-4779-3

TABLE OF CONTENTS

LIST OF FIGURES

LIST OF TABLES

About the Author

Savvakis C. Savvides is a former Senior Manager at the Cyprus Development Bank. He was Head of the Project Financing Division specialising in the evaluation and financing of capital investment projects. He has been a regular Visiting Lecturer on the Harvard Institute for International Development Program on Investment Appraisal and Management at Harvard University and on the Program on Investment Appraisal and Risk at the John Deutsch Institute for the Study of Economic Policy at Queen's University in Canada. He is the author of several publications on investment appraisal, risk analysis and the application of marketing and business strategy in project evaluation. He is also the developer of professional software for risk analysis and financial modelling, such as RiskEase, which is used worldwide by professionals and academics to assess project risk.

FOREWORD

There are four key areas in a capital investment evaluation that make for a professional appraisal of risk and return. First, a sound methodology for an economic cost-benefit analysis of capital investment projects is a prerequisite for a comprehensive appraisal. There is consensus among academics and professional practitioners regarding the practice and application of an economic cost-benefit analysis in the appraisal of capital investment projects and in determining economic viability. Second, one further needs to use a sound and robust integrated financial model which correctly and prudently applies the methodology of cost-benefit analysis. Third, to structure the projection parts of such a model, one needs to do an analysis of the market and the competitive data to be projected in the appraisal. This phase, which unfortunately is not given enough attention in practice, is essential for projecting growth patterns of key variables in a consistent and coherent manner. A good and thoughtful strategic marketing analysis is also key for the fourth stage, which entails subjecting the financial projections to risk analysis using Monte Carlo Simulation methodology. Finally, the above analysis should lead to the derivation of the project's risk profile and how it may impact the various stakeholders and financiers of the project. This paves the way for an appropriate and fair agreement for a financing structure which shares the risks fairly among the stakeholders and apportions them to those that can best mitigate and manage them. This book addresses each of these aspects of a high-quality investment appraisal to enhance the capital investment decision.

ACKNOWLEDGMENTS

Over my career, there have been many who have inspired, encouraged, and helped me along. I can only mention a few. First is Peter Spillard who was my professor at Lancaster University, while I was doing my Master's degree. Peter believed in me and advised me to explore my potential through hard work and by seeking and adopting the new. Another mentor in my life was John Joannides who as the General Manager of the Cyprus Development Bank, gave me a platform through which to develop my skills and competencies in assessing risk and return in the field. Professor Glenn P. Jenkins at Harvard University and later at Queen's University in Canada, was perhaps the one who has, like no other, worked with me for a period of nearly 40 years encouraging me to write and publish as well as to develop my risk analysis software. I would surely not have achieved much without having Glenn as an associate, colleague and last, but not least, friend. There are many others who have helped and inspired me along the way. Special mention should be made to Dr Graham Glenday of Harvard and later of Duke University with whom we have conceived together the conceptual foundations of what I have developed as RiskEase© Monte Carlo Simulation software.

I wish to thank my good friend Dr George M. Georgiou for edits and very helpful comments. Thanks, are also due to Marios Kourtellis for proofreading the manuscript. All errors are, of course, mine.

PREFACE

This volume on Risk Analysis in Project Appraisal is a synthesis of the outstanding scientific and professional work undertaken by Savvakis C. Savvides over a period of forty years. It has been my privilege to have been able to discuss with him many of the ideas presented here on numerous occasions.

The book deals with the assessment of risk and return in capital investment and decisions and has as its focus the four fundamental analytical components of investment appraisal. They are: (1) the appropriate integrated financial model to use in undertaking such an appraisal; (2) the use of a formal market, or demand and supply, analysis to determine the need and competitiveness of the proposed project; (3) the steps one must take to prepare and analyse the results of a quantitative risk analysis using Monte Carlo simulation techniques; and (4) the analysis of the risk and returns for real investments particularly in project finance situations, which is then contrasted with the traditional analysis of the relationship between risk and return for financial assets.

This volume should be studied carefully by everyone engaged in the appraisal of real investments, and especially those interested in learning the fundamentals of project finance decision making. It is well grounded in economic fundamentals as well as the financial context in which such investment decisions are made.

Savvakis Savvides has been one of the modern-day pioneers in quantitative risk analysis of real investments. About 40 years ago he developed one of the first computer software packages for the quantitative analysis of risk using Monte Carlo simulations. This software has been continuously updated and today represents the state of the art in this field. His skills in finance, economics and quantitative risk analysis are reinforced by decades of practical experience from structuring successful project finance investments.

Several chapters in the book have circulated as working papers. He has used this opportunity to share and refine his ideas and recommendations with feedback from academics and professionals engaged in the appraisal of such projects.

This book is straight forward to read and is beautifully illustrated. It is both a textbook for those new to the field and a reference book for the practitioners. It can be highly recommended for both audiences.

Dr Glenn P. Jenkins, Professor of Economics Queen's University, Canada, and Institute Fellow Emeritus Harvard University.

I. Introduction

What I find intriguing, and at the same time rather challenging, is how we go about in trying to predict what may happen in the future. Professionally, I found myself having to make such assessments in the normal course of executing my duties, initially as an analyst and subsequently from various other posts with the Cyprus Development Bank, but also in other instances in my career where I was involved in the appraisal of risk and return in new capital investments and project finance ventures. I was also deeply involved with this in an academic capacity, mostly as a visiting lecturer at Harvard University and later at Queen's University in Canada.

I was lucky to have had exposure to this fascinating field from both academic and practitioner vantage points. This helped me keep focus on the application of the theory and at the same time to benefit immensely from the insights obtained in real life projects. My involvement in a professional capacity in project finance and credit risk assessment enabled me to constantly enhance and enrich my understanding of its theoretical foundations but also to methodically be seeking to develop practical ways and tools for better applying the theory. This has led me to become actively involved in software development and the publishing of computer applications by providing a platform for practitioners to apply these concepts and methodologies to assess risk and return in their field of activities.

Figure 1 outlines the book structure. As it happens, these are also the areas that I have had major contributions in this field for well over three decades. I published, taught, and most importantly practiced what I preached in many real projects as Head of Project Financing of the Cyprus Development Bank in all the areas and aspects of project finance. Although I do of course touch upon the methodology of cost-benefit analysis, as it is at the core of capital investment decisions, I have tried to focus on the parts that complement a good appraisal and the areas that I happened to have had a significant involvement in the field.

Figure 1 - Evaluation of capital investment projects and the assessment of risk

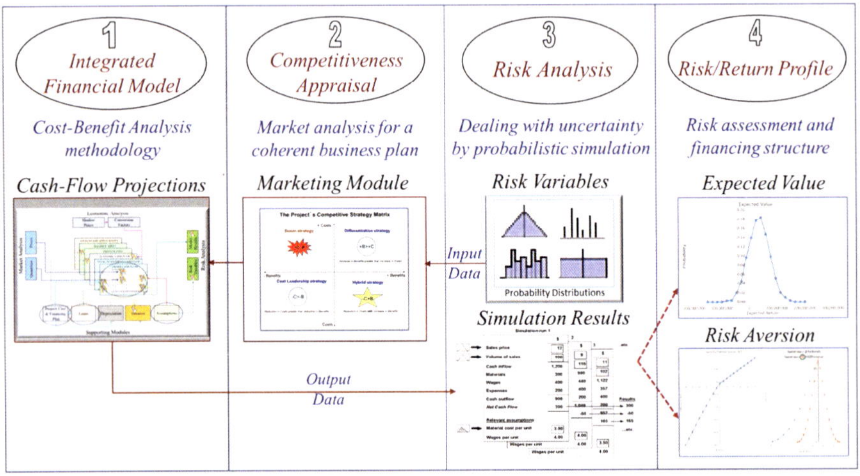

In the first section of the book, following a brief introduction of the methodology for applying the Monte Carlo methodology in investment appraisal, I present and discuss the *Integrated Financial Model* which fills the huge need for a reliable but simple and yet complete financial model for compiling and projecting pertinent cash flows, rather than a very detailed one as is the established practice by consultants and other practitioners. In addition, the need to deal effectively with *the correlation problem* arising during a simulation (as presented and discussed in Chapter IV) is mitigated and contained by using *growth pattern projections.* The few key parameters driving these consistent projections which can then be defined as risk variables in a Monte Carlo application.

When considering the past, the more detail one provides then often the better. This is because the past is cast in stone and exists as a certainty. But when projecting into the future, too much detail obstructs rather than aids our understanding of what is possible to happen. In my experience with the appraisal of many major project-finance ventures when consulting advice was sought, almost all ended up as examples where "***more is less***". Especially where the detailed data thus gathered was not used as inputs to a simple but comprehensive financial model for projecting consistent scenarios. Taking a high-definition picture of the past is certainly not the best way to contemplate and evaluate what may happen in the future as regards a capital investment project. A simple but methodologically correct integrated financial model is therefore imperative for a good and pertinent appraisal.

The second section complements and, most importantly, adds substance to the quantitative analysis of the financial model. It concerns the methodology for applying an appropriate market analysis and assessment of the competitive environment of the project. *It discusses* the key driving forces in the market the project is to operate and is vital in undertaking a meaningful strategic analysis. This is presented in chapter III on the *Market and Competitiveness Appraisal.* These neglected but important aspects of investment appraisal and the assessment of risk and return evolve around two papers I wrote and have taught extensively. These concepts have been published as Harvard Development Discussion papers, Savvakis (1988) and Savvakis (1990) and it is an area I studied well at university and have also practised in almost everything I was involved with in my professional career.

Chapter IV is about the actual application of *risk analysis* using the Monte Carlo Simulation methodology in investment appraisal projects. This section presents the methodology as published in my paper on "Risk Analysis in Investment Appraisal" in the late 1980s and published in the *Project Appraisal Journal* in 1994. The article was the conceptual background on which risk analysis software such as *RiskEase*© were developed to enable one to apply in simple and clear manner the Monte Carlo Simulation methodology in capital investment appraisal.

The last part of the book is on *what risk really is (Chapter V)* and how it may be measured and applied in capital investment and project finance decisions (Chapters V and VI). This is something I wanted to write about for a long time as many professors and colleagues with whom I have discussed the issue were not at ease in accepting that "*volatility*" is a good description or even an adequate measure of what is risk in capital investment. It proposes the uses of expected value and, more specifically, expected loss as a measure of risk and as outlined in the 1994 paper and applied through probabilistic appraisal using Monte Carlo simulation software. Further, through this methodology (and software such as *RiskEase*©) it is also possible to undertake risk aversion analysis and consider the capacity of a given project to meet and satisfy investor risk preferences.

Finally (Chapter VII and VIII) some actual case studies will be cited as specimens of how the concepts presented in the book may be applied in real life project finance. These include an example of how this type of holistic and all-inclusive analysis may be applied in the evaluation of a guarantee in a Public-Private Partnership (PPP) concession agreement.

This book is an attempt to put forward the essence of what I have come to learn and understand through research and practice about how to assess risk and return and in making better capital investment and financing decisions.

Whose cash flows?

Before one can attempt to answer the question regarding the need for economic evaluation for a capital investment project, it is imperative to ask first "*whose economic viability*"? No matter how well one tries to evaluate return and assess risk in a new capital investment, economic viability is and looks different from the perspective of the various stakeholders. In effect, cash-flows projected for the whole nation (the *"Economy's"* perspective and adjusted to reflect economic prices) are different from those of the *"Owner"* of the project or from those of the *"Total Investment"* perspective where it assumed that the project is solely funded by equity and therefore does not include loans received (as inflows) and repaid (as outflows) in the projected cash flows (as is the structure of the projected cash flows from the Owner's viewpoint).

There are several other cash flows that can be compiled and projected as they refer to various parties and stakeholders involved in a capital investment project. When one talks about the need for a new capital investment project to be economically viable, it is usually regarding a project evaluation from the economy's perspective. This is a necessary but not sufficient condition for undertaking a public sector or a private-public-partnership (PPP). For such a project to be implemented the *Owner,* and often other *key stakeholders,* should also expect a positive risk and return profile. This is imperative before committing funds and other economic resources to a capital investment project.

Cost-Benefit Analysis and Economic Development

The need for economic viability however is sometimes disregarded by politicians who are often keen not to have their pet projects subjected to independent appraisals, which may cause their rejection. Moreover, politicians, but also people generally, tend to confuse the inflow of funds into an economy with what is economic development. What they tend not to appreciate is that it is not the funding but the actual *use of funds* that can bring about sustainable economic development and welfare. As pointed out by many economists, the uncontrolled inflow of money into an economy can result in making it worse off. The banks must position this money in the form of loans to generate an income from the accruing interest. A huge and abnormal inflow of deposits in a country simply encourages the banks to embark on collateral lending rather than through prudent assessment of viability and repayment capability. Politicians, lawyers, and many other intermediaries who benefit from having wealthy customers improperly argue that any investment is a good one and that the economy becomes better off by having funds injected into it (as deposits or in purchasing real estate). This, however, could not be any further from the truth. There are many examples where it drives an economy and its economic agents into an excessive and unsustainable debt burden (both private and public).

Economics is about using economic resources to maximise the welfare of a society. To move an economy closer to that optimum point of economic welfare, it is necessary to employ capital and labour and other factors of production such as land closer to their most efficient uses. However, to successfully accelerate the pace of economic development, in addition to increasing the levels of employment and attaining high efficiencies for the factors of economic production, it is also necessary to yield a good return on capital. This in effect means that a project scrutinised through a cost-benefit analysis test should have a positive net present value (where the projected net cash flow discounted at the opportunity cost of capital is greater than zero).

The assessment of risk and return in capital investment

As mentioned above there are four key areas in a capital investment evaluation that make for a good and sound appraisal of risk and return, as illustrated in the Figure 1. The methodology of cost benefit analysis for capital investment projects is of course a prerequisite for a sound appraisal[1]. There is consensus regarding the practice and application of cost benefit analysis in the appraisal of capital investment projects and in determining economic viability. But although the correct methodology is necessary it is not always sufficient to facilitate the decision of whether to invest.

One further needs to have a sound and robust ***integrated financial model*** which correctly and prudently applies the methodology of cost-benefit

[1] Harberger, Arnold C., and Glenn P. Jenkins 2000, Jenkins, G.P., 1998

analysis. Secondly, it is also fundamental to structure the projection parts of such a model only after first doing the serious homework on the market and competitive analysis data to be projected in the appraisal. This phase, which is not given sufficient attention in practice, is essential to reveal the driving parameters and to project growth patterns for key variables in a consistent and coherent manner. A good and thoughtful marketing analysis is also key when subjecting the financial projections to risk analysis using Monte Carlo Simulation. Last, but not least, the above analysis should lead to the derivation of the project's risk profile and how it may impact the various stakeholders and financiers of the project. This facilitates an appropriate agreement for a financing structure and for sharing of the risks among all stakeholders.

What is risk and can it be measured?

But why do we even bother to assess risk and return one may ask? We surely cannot predict the future. Anyone that argues otherwise is either fooling himself or trying to sell you something. We cannot predict the future. Period! Be that as it may, there is an underlying need to make the best we can of what we may know or can gather to guide us in making a studied and better considered decision. And it is not a "Yes/No" decision either. The ability to model and understand risk and return often facilitates an improved formulation and leads to such arrangements to better deal with risks as these may arise during the life of the project. So, the purpose of going through a diligent and thoughtful appraisal of return and risk is to raise the metric of decision making and to understand risks as well as to better appreciate the competitive strengths (and weaknesses) of a proposed investment project. An enhanced understanding of the capital investment project and its risk and return profile even allows for a reformulation to make it more robust and better equipped to compete successfully in its targeted market. In addition, this process also facilitates the arrangement of an appropriate financing solution. Equity participation and debt exposure may therefore be adapted according to the ability of each party to manage and cope with specific project risks. Given appropriate expertise and software tools, such methodological scrutiny of new capital investment projects also contributes for a better allocation of resources and hence fosters economic development.

Whose risk and whose return?

A question left relatively untouched in the application of economic analysis in capital investment projects is that which is usually referred to by Harberger (1971) as the *third postulate of Welfare Economics*. Simply put, it is assumed that economic value is the result of net present value of the costs and benefits in an economy *irrespective of who gains and who loses*. This is largely a useful assumption as it enables one to calculate the net effect of any given investment on a country without getting entangled into issues of inequality and subjective estimations of welfare. However, although it facilitates a generic project evaluation methodology it is a somewhat of an unrealistic assumption to assert that as that long as the Economic net present value is positive one cannot question inequality aspects and transfers of wealth within the country. This assumption, as it will be demonstrated in the Motorway project sometimes results in the absurd conclusion that in a Public-Private Partnership project the tax-payer can pick up the bill for supporting a private entrepreneur with any amount as long as that particular capital investment project is deemed to have a positive net present value from the Economy's perspective. In its current state, the analysis extends to the point of constructing what is called as Stakeholder Analysis, see Jenkins, Koo, Harberger (1991). This is calculated and presented as supplementary to the core appraisal and shows how the Economic NPV is made up by indicating how various parties involved directly or indirectly in a capital investment project are assessed to be affected by it (who gains and who loses).

The detachment of risk from return

Risk and return are the twin cylinders of the engine driving a free capitalist market. There is *no such thing as a return without risk*. Risk is simply the ambiguity that encompasses an entrepreneurial investment project as its future cash flows cannot be determined with certainty. Economic development is attained by *taking on risks* that are *part and parcel* of *productive capital investment* projects. Where risk is systematically detached from return the result is not *wealth creation* but rather *wealth extraction and transfer of assets*.

In the times we live in there are two key words people understand and very often interpret wrongly. The word "*investment*" and the word "*risk*". Funding and earning a return (rent) does not necessarily constitute a productive investment that builds up the real economy. To add to the existing welfare of a society the project should be economically viable. If it does not fulfil these conditions often it leads to a transfer of existing assets (frequently real property) and may be better described as wealth extraction. The total assets in the economy do not change; only the ownership does. In the times we live in, this is further facilitated by a loose world financial market and a failing banking system whereby banks provide on-balance sheet loans, or better known as collateral lending, without a proper assessment of repayment capability (Savvides 2019).

The second big fallacy in finance is what investment risk is really and how it may be evaluated and measured. It is not volatility of stocks but rather the probability weighted negative return (expected loss) that is undertaken by various stakeholders in a capital investment project. This is taken up in detail in the section on "Risk and return Revisited (risk through the looking glass)" later in this book (Savvides 2022b).

II. The Integrated Financial Model

Understanding and mastering the correct cost-benefit methodology and applying Monte Carlo simulation is a necessary but not a sufficient condition for a proper and sound appraisal of risk and return of a capital investment project. The methodology, if applied correctly, will allow one to include and formulate the correct variables and thereby to draw the correct inferences and conclusions regarding the message they may convey. But by itself, this is rarely enough or adequate for the appraisal of risk and return.

When one is confronted with a decision about the future, projecting in a similar manner as we account for the past by gathering as much detail as we can is not an advantage. Quite the contrary in fact. When considering how a business plan may evolve one can only hope that as the future unfolds it will be close to what was assumed in the projections. But, unlike the past, as the future reveals itself, we can always adapt our actions and policies along the way to better manage some of the risks and how these may affect the outcome of a given project. This is why we apply probabilistic analysis to a base case projection using the Monte Carlo simulation methodology. Monte Carlo simulation is a methodology that allows us to map, or sketch out, the spectrum of possibilities of what it is reasonable to expect based on the probabilistic assumptions made in a projected financial model. What we expect is that the analysis will enable us to better understand and gauge the impact of specific risks that stakeholders and financiers involved in a capital investment project may be called to undertake.

To achieve this, we do not need a complex financial model and to gather every detail from the past to forecast the possible outcomes for evaluating a given project. This, in any case, is not why an appraisal of risk and return is undertaken. We do not try to predict or even guess the future. We look and analyse the past only to the extent that it enables us to understand how factors that relate to our specific project work and then use this knowledge to create a simplified but elaborate enough model to help us take prudent risk mitigation and management as well as investment financing decisions. Though a thoughtful and correctly applied probabilistic analysis in the evaluation of risk and return we enhance and raise the metric of decision making in undertaking and funding capital investments.

To facilitate this process, it is useful to have available a well-tested integrated financial model which applies the correct cost-benefit analysis.

One such adaptable, coherent, and easy to use financial model is the Integrated Financial Model© by *Savvakis C. Savvides*. This was created and tested after many years of expertise of the author in project finance and corporate lending appraisals as well as from teaching and writing about the subject, including the development of several related software. The model is designed so that it offers the user the following benefits:

1. To be set up easily and quickly.
2. To be coherent and comprehensive.
3. To be adaptable with very few changes.
4. To be usable for any type or size of project.
5. To be well and truly integrated.
6. To be driven by a manageable number of important parameters and to include and accommodate the simple use of a specially designed forecasting Excel Add-In which allows the easy and coherent projections of growth patterns.
7. To be ready for Risk Analysis using Monte Carlo simulation software (see RiskEase in Appendix).
8. To produce reports of financial cash flow projections from the perspective of various stakeholders, including the owner of the project, the total investment perspective or and to be easily expandable so as application of economic analysis.
9. The Model can also be quickly set up to be used for screening promising or to discard poor and non-viable projects.
10. Last, but not least, the model can be attached as a front end to very large and elaborate workbooks to make sense of their useful, but often not so well integrated, content of data.

The Integrated Financial Model (IFM) was built to enable the sound and reliable appraisal and funding of proposed capital investment projects. The norm before the creation of the IFM was to construct from scratch basically a new financial model containing all the details and data of the project at hand. There were two problems with this approach: it takes a long time to prepare and even longer to have it audited and tested so that it could be relied on to base such serious decisions.

Armed with the experience of many such endeavours and with the knowledge gathered relating to what would constitute a reliable tool for undertaking a risk and return analysis an adaptable but reliable model was built. This was constantly improved and enhanced with every new project. The IFM is rather unique for two reasons. The first is that that it is both simple and comprehensive. It does cover all aspects of a cost-benefit application and produces all the required reports. The second which is equally, if not more important, relates to the word "integrated" as it is driven only by the few key parameters that are entered by the user. It is possible to set up the Project Cost and Financing Plan quickly and easily (a requirement for any capital investment project assessment), enter any existing or completely new project with all the settings required, add some key parameters in the Assumptions sheet and prepare it for using a Growth Patterns Projection template to project forecasts and then link the results to the Cash flow Owner sheet and so on. The IFM builds up a picture of what the project is sketching out to be and as soon as all the parameters are set all the reports are ready (as illustrated in Figure 2).

Figure 2 - The Integrated Financial Model

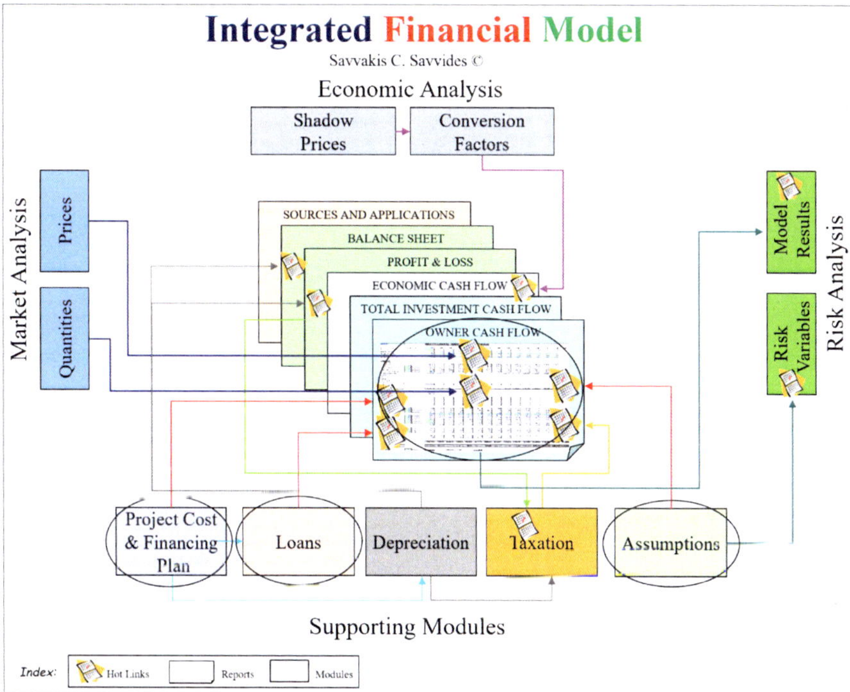

A third and very important aspect of the IFM is that it is risk analysis ready. It is imperative to have such an integrated financial model in place and one that is driven by a few key parameters ready to apply on a meaningful risk analysis using the Monte Carlo simulation methodology. The IFM is a very sophisticated engine under the hood but also one that is rather simple to use.

But one can get an appreciation of how it is employed to enhance the understanding of risk and return from the examples presented.

As mentioned above, the more detail we provide when looking into the past the clearer the picture becomes. This is what accountants do in fact when they gather data and compile a historical account. However, when looking forward into what may happen in the future more detail is not always better. This is because the future has not happened yet. As obvious as this may sound, in practice experts and consultants often provide as much detail as possible usually by gathering and putting together in a complex and sophisticated spreadsheet a collection of data assembled from various historical sources. Such as past records of a company or its competitors, quantities and prices for many similar products, market shares and even detailed descriptions of markets by regions and types of customers or supplier. In fact, they approach the future the same way an accountant would record, construe, and then report the historical past.

Contrary to general belief the future cannot be predicted. What may be forthcoming, at best, can only be better understood and appreciated. It cannot be reported or accounted for the way we look at the past because it has not happened yet. But there is a huge upside. While you cannot change one iota of the past one can learn and adapt and adjust what may happen to a project in the future. As illustrated in Figure 3 by identifying and projecting the key parameters through the prism of a reliable financial model we may reveal a blurred spectrum of how the future may unfold. This at best can only be understood probabilistically. Possible outcomes are weighed against their probabilities within a Monte Carlo simulation framework.

The assessment of what can be expected from a proposed capital investment is therefore always in terms of expected value of return. The sum of negative returns (below 0 NPV) in a simulation multiplied by their probabilities is what we term as Expected Loss from the investment while the positive returns (above 0 NPV) multiplied by their respective probabilities make up the Expected Gain from the investment. Risk is not "volatility" as perceived by someone on the floor of a Stock Exchange but rather the probability weighted expected returns. The "expected loss" and "expected gain" concepts together make up the expected value of return of the project as whole.

Figure 3 - Risk through the prism of a financial model subjected to simulation

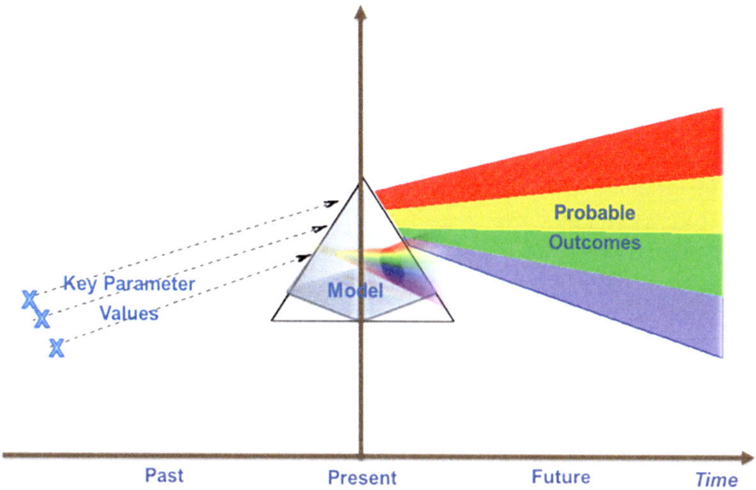

There is a huge gap between how practitioners in general apply the cost benefit methodology focusing on too much detail and not *the substance* in appraising a capital investment. The mistake is to try to picture the future in every detail as one would when looking at the historical past. Rather than enhancing the understanding of what drives a project and how it may be successful in a competitive market environment, such an approach only succeeds in adding to the confusion and it is a poor base on which one can pertinently make thoughtful and sound capital investment decisions about risk and return.

The future is by its nature uncertain

If there is something we know for certain is that there is nothing certain regarding the future. We simply cannot foresee the future. There is no crystal ball that can show us even a mere glimpse of what will take place at some time in the future. The future is by definition probabilistic. The appraisal of any future project at best can only enhance our understanding of what we may reasonably expect from as the future unfolds and how it may affect our plans. We can only learn from the past to gain a good idea of what we may expect to happen if we repeat such actions at a future time. But in an ever-changing world even that is not a given. And yet, we continue to project our assumptions for a given business plan as if we expect them to take place with absolute certainty. Moreover, we also take as given that the outcomes of a projected financial model will be as thus calculated. In effect, however, whether we realise this or not, we attach to each projected input in a financial model a single-value probability distribution. In other words, we presume that all we project will happen with 100% probability and with no possible deviation. This is why the outcomes projected are also deterministic and presented as certainties. In effect this means that if we were to use Monte Carlo simulation methodology to run probabilistic scenarios using this certainty equivalent single-value probability distributions for each risk variable, the scenarios generated will all be identical and the same.

We can obviously improve our understanding of risk and what may happen in the future of any such financial model of a projected business plan by relaxing the single-value probability certainty equivalent assumption for those parameters we consider to be risk variables. The result is, of course, that we end up with multi-value probability distributions for the outcomes in the projected model which is subjected to Monte Carlo simulation.

A Monte Carlo simulation can, and sadly sometimes is, used a mechanical rather than in a manner through which to gain a better understanding of a given project. One that merely gazes at the results arrived at from any of the two approaches possible will hardly be able to tell the difference. Hence, the need to research and write about how to use Monte Carlo simulation risk analysis so that the application of the methodology truly enhances one's understanding of the project and helps make better capital investment decisions.

The assessment of risk and return in capital investment entails more than just the projection of single value expected revenues and costs. One needs to be applying the correct cost-benefit analysis methodology but also to employ an integrated financial model ([1] in Figure 1) where the details take second place to the competitive strategy of the project in its defined relevant market and targeted customers. This is done through a coherent competitiveness appraisal ([2] in Figure 1). The integrated financial model is also a necessary condition for projecting and maintaining consistency in one's assumptions when switching from the deterministic base value case to the probabilistic multi-value risk variables in the context of a Monte Carlo simulation process ([3] in Figure 1). Finally, one needs to assess risk in the correct context of expected value ([4] in Figure 1) rather than in the historical volatility measures that are typically gathered and viewed from the floor of a stock exchange. A prudent risk assessment will also form the basis for arriving to an appropriate financing structure for a viable capital investment project.

What is project risk and how to measure it

What is real risk and how may it be measured and applied in capital investment and project finance decisions? Many project finance professionals are not at ease in accepting that volatility is a good or even an adequate description of what is capital investment risk. It is proposed that the use of expected value and more specifically expected loss as a measure of risk and as outlined in my published paper on Risk Analysis be applied through pertinent probabilistic appraisal using software such as *RiskEase*[2]. Through this methodology it is also possible to undertake risk aversion analysis and consider the capacity of a given project to meet and satisfy investor risk preferences.

When we describe the past, the more detail we provide the more accurate we become. When we try to predict the future however, the more detail we attempt to carry forward from the past the less likely we will be to capture the essence of what may happen and to properly assess the risks. The future is uncertain. And no matter what people may claim, no one can predict the future. The best we can do is to assess in probabilistic terms on what we may expect to happen with respect to a given business plan we may have in mind to implement. Moreover, as illustrated in Figure 4, the longer into the future we look the wider the margins of uncertainty become and the probability distribution of the outcome we try to gauge and measure.

Probabilistic analysis using Monte Carlo simulation is a necessary but not sufficient condition to properly assess a capital investment. To analyse and assess project risk one needs to have:

A simple, coherent, and fully **integrated financial model** which:

- applies the correct **cost-benefit analysis** methodology
- accommodates a **competitiveness appraisal**, and
- reliably **facilitates probabilistic risk analysis** (remains consistent and maintains its predictive ability in a Monte Carlo Simulation test).

---

[2] Using *RiskEase*© software, by RiskEase Ltd (www.riskease.com).

Figure 4 - The Assessment of Risk is Probabilistic

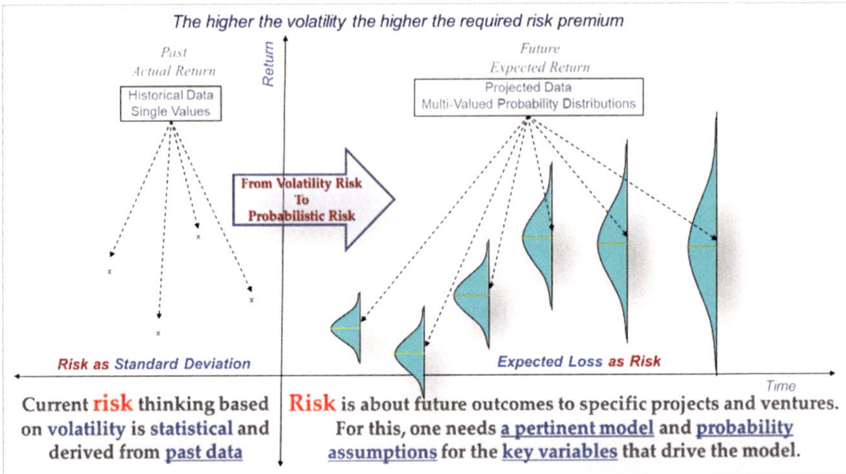

Therefore, before applying a sound and all-encompassing Monte Carlo simulation risk analysis, it is imperative that one employs an adaptable but fully *integrated financial model*. There are three essential requirements for this to happen which will be presented and discussed below:

1. It should apply the correct ***cost-benefit analysis*** *methodology and*
2. *Be* ***complete*** *covering all constituent parts of a comprehensive appraisal but remain simple and easily driven within an* ***integrated financial model***.
3. It must be modelled in a manner so that coherent and consistent scenarios will be generated during a simulation. To achieve this one needs to employ ***growth patterns*** *and* ***correlation settings*** *for the key risk variables*.

Cost-Benefit Analysis

The project net cash flow (benefits – costs) typically shows negative net cash flow for the initial years (as it is mostly the cost of the capital investment) and positive ones following the operational years as is resembled in the example in Figure 5. There is also a residual value collection at the assumed end of the life of the project.

Figure 5 - Project Net Cash Flow Profile

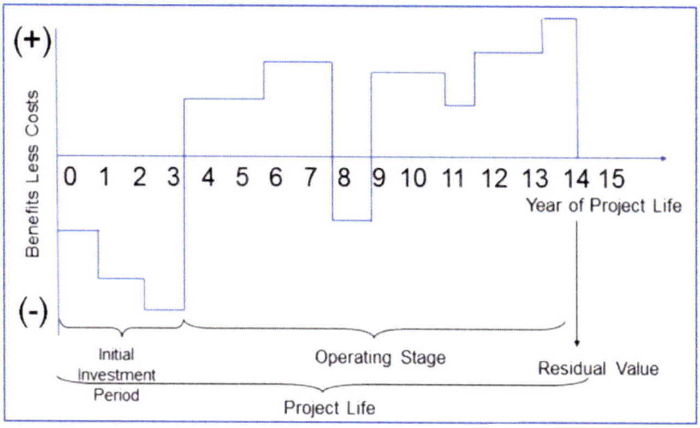

The Cash Flow projections can be drafted from different perspectives as they affect various stakeholders in a capital investment.

Project Stakeholders and Alternative Points of View

In a capital investment project, there are often more than one stakeholder involved. Particularly in capital investments for the public sector or in Public Private Partnerships (PPPs) one must evaluate the return and risks that may arise to different parties. It is therefore imperative to distinguish this and evaluate the cost and benefits of a planned investment that may accrue to the main stakeholders. The most common cash flow perspectives are:

a. Point of view of **Owner** (includes loans and repayments in the cash flow)

b. Point of view of **Total investment** (or *Banker's point of view*) which assumes that capital investment is financed completely through equity.

c. Point of view of **Economy**

Other examples of project perspectives that one may construct cash flows for are the government budget view, suppliers of inputs view and downstream processor's view. A well-balanced stakeholders' analysis of the different perspectives will highlight where and to whom the benefits and costs may accrue to. It can also form the basis on which the risks may be allocated to those parties involved in the project that are best fit to manage them (as in Figure 6).

Figure 6 - Analysis of Investment from Different Viewpoints

Analysis →	Financial				Economic	
Viewpoints:	Total Investment (Project) (A)		Owner (B)		Country (C)	
Year:	0	1	0	1	0	1
Receipts		400		400		440
Operating Cost		-140		-140		-150
Equipment	-1000	950	-1000	950	-1100	1045
Operating Subsidy		50		50		
Taxes		-100		-100		
Loan			500	-500		
Interest				-50		
Environ. Externality						-190
Opp. Cost of Land	-30	-30	-30	-30	-30	-30
Net Resource Flow	-1030	1130	-530	580	-1130	1115

More specifically the following will be referred to as they relate to the Cash Flow projections:

Residual Values (Cash Inflows)

- Buildings, Electromechanical, Furniture and Fittings, etc.
- Land

Assets Values (Cash Outflows)

- Buildings, Electromechanical, Furniture and Fittings, etc.
- Interest During Construction
- Land

Adjustments for **Working Capital**

- Accounts Receivable
- Accounts Payable
- Cash at hand

Outcomes (*Model Results*) of Financial Model

- Net Cash Flow
- Discounting Cash Flow: NPV and IRR
- Debt Service Coverage Ratios (Annual)
- Debt Service Coverage Ratios (Accumulated)

Cash Flow Statement Structure and Derivation

The Cost Benefit Analysis methodology is well-documented and is being applied for over 60 years effectively worldwide to identify viable capital investment projects. The Cash Flow from Owner's perspective is the fundamental core view as it gathers all inputs in a financial model and forms the basis from which to generate the cash flow for the "Total Investment" or "Economy's" perspectives. The Total Investment view is essentially the Owner's perspective cash flow without the loans as inflows and the repayment in terms of interest and principal as outflows as it is assumed that the investment is wholly equity financed. The Total investment perspective cash flow projections can then subsequently used as a basis to construct the Economy's Cash Flow which entails the calculation of Economic shadow prices [1].

The Cash Flow Owner's perspective (CF-Owner) integrates the inputs of a Financial Model. As such it will be discussed and used to demonstrate the *Integrated Financial Model* (IFM). It connects and links to all other inputs and supporting modules. More specifically the settings for the following items in the derivation of a Cash Flow Statement will be referred to as discussed (Figure 7).

Figure 7 - Cash Flow Owners Perspective Template

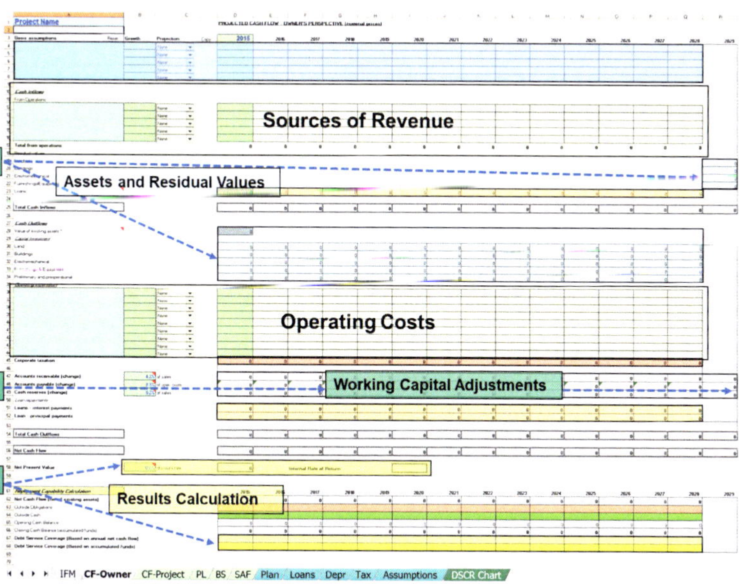

Assets and Residual Values

- Buildings, Electromechanical, Furniture and Fittings, etc.
- Land

Figure 8 - Project Assets and Residual Values

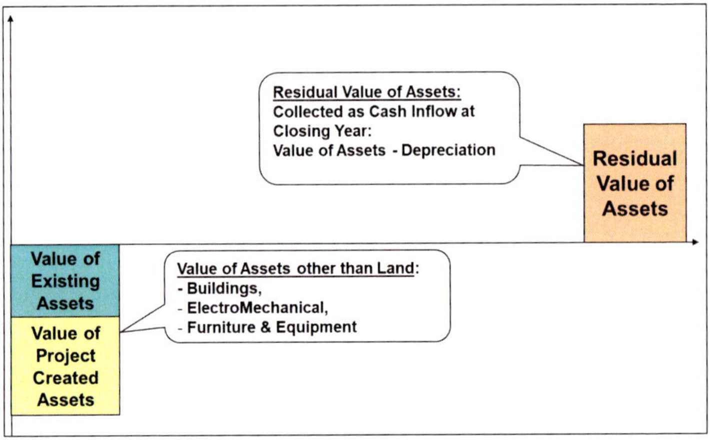

The Value of the Land must be "collected" as residual value at the end of the projection period at the same real cost it went into the cash flows as cost at the beginning of the period. In nominal terms, adjusted for inflation only (as illustrated in Figure 8). Similarly for Working Capital (as illustrated in Figure 9).

Adjustments for Working Capital

- Accounts Receivable
- Accounts Payable
- Cash at hand

Outcomes (Model Results) of Financial Model

- Net Cash Flow
- Discounting Cash Flow: NPV and IRR
- Debt Service Coverage Ratios (Annual)
- Debt Service Coverage Ratios (Accumulated)

Figure 9 - Working Capital Cash Flow Adjustments

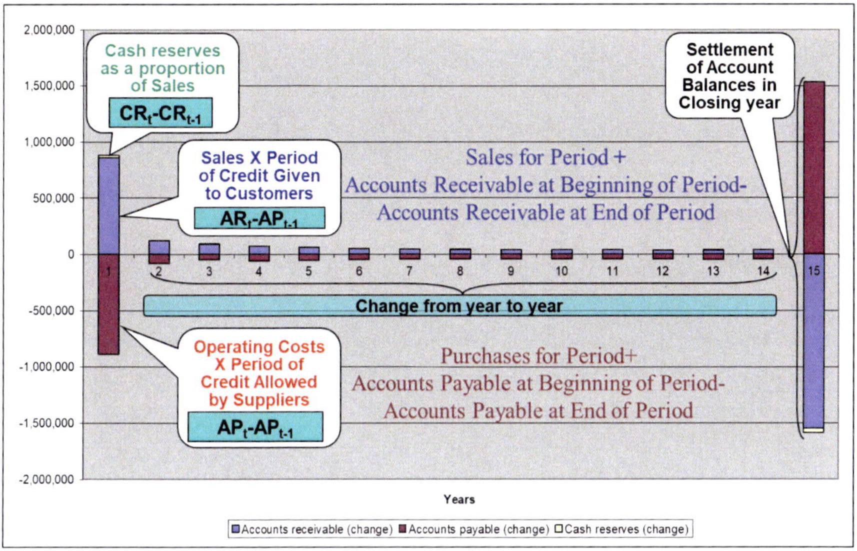

Figures 10 and 11 demonstrate how the most common results in a cash flow projection are calculated.

Figure 10 - CF-Owner Report Outputs (Model Results)

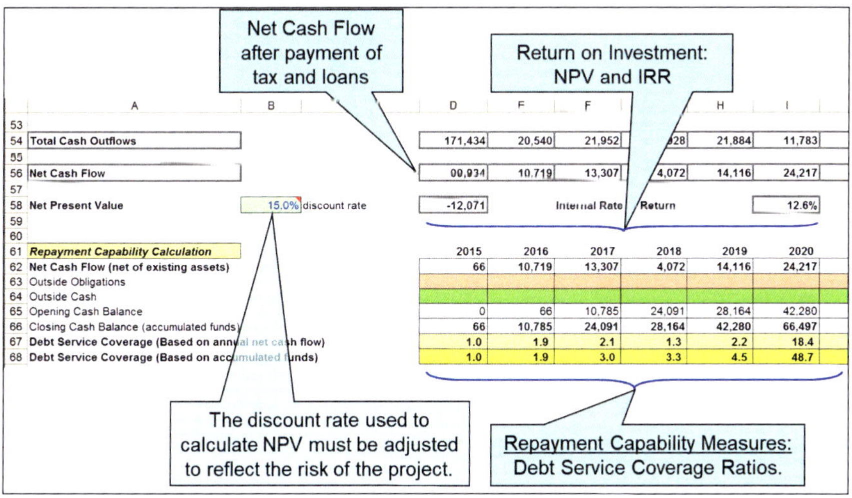

Figure 11 - Discounting and calculating NPV and IRR

Net Present Value (NPV)

$$\textbf{NPV} = B\text{-}C + \frac{B\text{-}C}{(1+r)^{\wedge 1}} + \frac{B\text{-}C}{(1+r)^{\wedge 2}} + \frac{B\text{-}C}{(1+r)^{\wedge 3}} + \frac{B\text{-}C}{(1+r)^{\wedge 4}}$$

Example of Discounting (10% Discount Rate)

Year	0	1	2	3	4
Net Cash Flow	-1000	200	300	350	1440

$$PV_{0.1}^{0} = -1000 + \frac{200}{1.1} + \frac{300}{(1.1)^2} + \frac{350}{(1.1)^3} + \frac{1440}{(1.1)^4}$$

NPV 676.25 = -1000.00 + 181.82 + 247.93 + 262.96 + 983.54

Internal Rate of Return (IRR)

$$\textbf{IRR formula} = \sum_{t=0}^{n} \frac{B_t - C_t}{(1+K)^t} = 0$$

IRR is the discount rate (K) at which the present value of benefits are just equal to the present value of costs for the particular project.

Note: the IRR is a mathematical concept, not an economic or financial criterion

Finally, one should calculate the Debt Service Coverage Ratios (DSCR) which measure how well the project can cover its loan debt by paying the interest and principal at the year it becomes due. The Annual DSCR in effect calculates how much cash-flows generated by project activities in the current period are higher than the debt service (interest including fees + scheduled principal) that is due in the same period. The Accumulated DSCR adds up the cumulative available net cash flows for the same period. This is illustrated in Figure 12.

Interest during Construction

Any interest that is paid during the construction phase of a project. Interest paid during construction period is often not deductible immediately as an expense. When is not immediately deductible as an expense it is added to the cost basis of the building instead and depreciable during operation of project for both taxation and financial reporting. For this reason, it is also known as capitalized interest.

Figure 12 - Debt Service Ratios

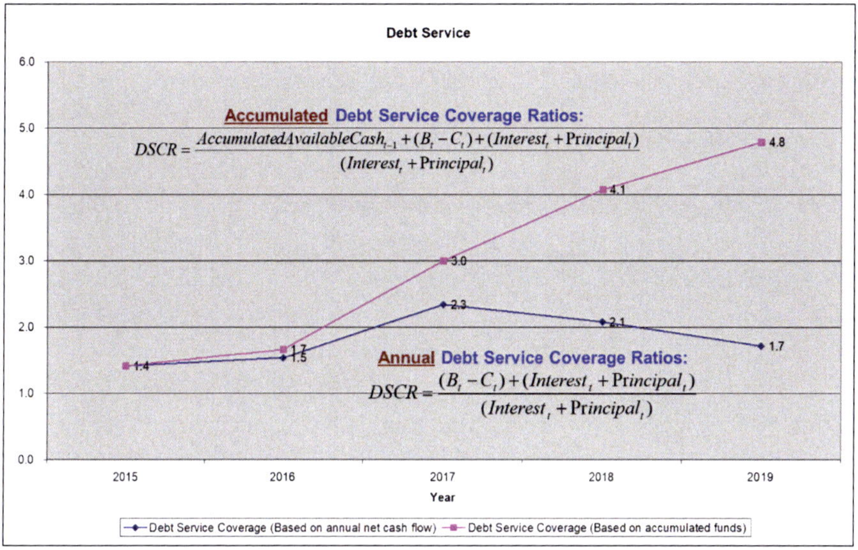

The integrated Financial Model

The Integrated Financial Model (IFM) emerged from the need to have a coherent, manageable, and fully integrated financial model which can be used in risk analysis of capital investment projects and in credit risk assessment applications by means of software that employ the Monte Carlo Simulation methodology (such as *RiskEase*© by RiskEase Ltd). The biggest obstacle one faces when attempting to relax the deterministic assumption behind single-value forecasts included in a cash flow projection to assess risk, and in fact in any other type of deterministic model, is the problem of correlation and how to deal with it. This in effect means that the financial model one builds must be able to withstand the effects of changes in the driving input parameters arising from the multi-value probabilistic assumptions made while also maintaining its internal consistency generating realistic scenarios. A generation of scenarios during a simulation using a model that that does not provide for this and does not adapt to these changing values during a simulation process is likely to lose its forecasting ability. In fact, if not dealt with sufficiently well it is likely to introduce enough bias in generating unrealistic projections that would probably outweigh any benefits to be derived from a Monte Carlo type of probabilistic assessment of risk.

To give an example, suppose one builds a model to evaluate the investment return of a new business venture. In fact, what he is putting together on a spreadsheet is one out of countless possible scenarios, which may be described as the base case scenario. To measure risk, one needs to explore in a consistent and systematic manner what the model predicts if there is, as it is expected, some variability in the basic parameters driving the business model. This is why an integrated and simple financial model is necessary as a tool to assess risk. Consider a typical forecasting spreadsheet model of prices and quantities as shown in the table below:

Table 1 - Projecting Cash Flows

Year	1	2	3	4	5
Number of widgets sold	100	120	130	140	150
Price	10	10	10	10	10
Revenue	1,000	1,200	1,300	1,400	1,500

The scenario shown in Table 1 above may be a reasonable one as a deterministic base case model. The analyst inputs some numbers in a spreadsheet as "best estimates" of quantities and prices to assess the amount of revenue he can expect from a business. Leaving aside for a while that sales depend on a host of other variables in the marketing mix of the company, such as the product features and its appeal to the targeted market, the advertising and promotion employed and the distribution channels available and even how competitive these products and prices are in the market (Savvides 2000), from a purely numerical point of view there is a real potential problem when one tries to replace deterministic with probabilistic values in the model. And that is that the inferred relationship in these parameters and values of a base case model will most likely be violated. The projection of sales of 120 units in year 2 in the above example is a reasonable one only if the attained sales in year 1 are 100 units (or thereabout). What happens however when we project that it is in fact possible that sales in year 1 can be as low as 50 units and as high as 150 units? Is the projection of 120 units in year 2 still pertinent if sales in year 1 are 70 units? Most probably not. There is an inferred relationship, or pattern if you prefer, that must be maintained when one relaxes the certainty equivalent assumptions for the purpose of assessing risk through simulation. The financial model should be capable to withstand such arduous tests. To take the above example one step further, are the prices which are assumed to be reasonable in the deterministic base case scenario still relevant when units sold in year 1 are way below expectations? Wouldn't a sounder and more coherent model adjust prices (and possibly other marketing mix variables – such as promotion) in year 2 and beyond to reflect the fact that sales are way below the viability threshold? Price in year 2 would most likely need to be reduced and promotion and distribution spending should increase (in a cost-effective manner) to generate a higher volume of sales in the future.

The point should be clear that the financial model must be maintaining its integrity and validity during the simulation process. To attain this, the model must be driven consistently through defining correlation settings but also realistic growth patterns and relationships between the key risk variables. Ergo, the need to put together an integrated financial model that applies the correct cost-benefit analysis methodology but also one that is also comprehensive in that it includes all modules and reports necessary in an appraisal of an investment. Moreover, it should be a financial model that uses *growth patterns* in the projection of key risk variables to generate consistent scenarios as these may arise from relaxing the deterministic assumptions and replacing them with multi-value probability distributions in the context of a Monte Carlo methodology. It should be a model that not only is *complete* and applying comprehensively the correct cost-benefit methodology but also easily *adaptable* and ready to be re-employed as a front-end in many different types and sizes of capital investment projects[3].

A complete, simple, and adaptable financial model

The Integrated Financial Model© (IFM) developed by RiskEase Ltd was prepared and tested in many projects, large and small and across many sectors, industrial, retail, infrastructure, small businesses. The philosophy of this approach is that no matter how much detail and complexity there is in a spreadsheet (usually prepared by big house name consultants) the IFM can be attached over other more detailed workbooks and with the appropriate links in place put order on top of chaos. The complex detailed model will in effect become a feeder data sheet to the more familiar and fully integrated financial model that sits on top of it when the two workbooks are put together. Analysts can further enhance and develop their skills in this respect through studying several case studies and by actual fieldwork in project finance and credit risk assessments. An overview of how the

[3] For an understanding of the framework for assessing credit risk in corporate lending read, [5] Savvides, Savvakis C. Corporate Lending and the Assessment of Credit Risk, Journal of Money, Investment and Banking, Issue 20, March 2011.

Integrated Financial Model (IFM) is applied is illustrated in Figure 13:

Figure 13 - Links to Source Sheets Updating the Cash Flow Owner Template

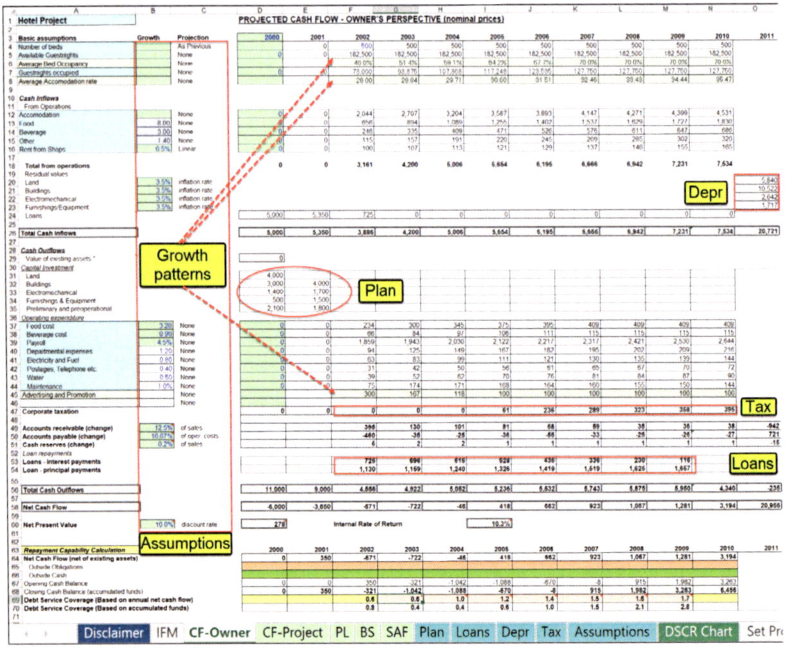

Growth patterns and correlations

The Investment Analysis Toolpak© is a collection of freeware add-in functions that one can use to define and project growth patterns in a financial model. They are included with RiskEase© Monte Carlo Simulation software and can be freely passed on with any workbook that uses them. They can easily be defined using only a few parameters as shown in Figure 14. They can then be copied and applied over the extent of periods in the projected cash flows.

Figure 14 - Growth Pattern Functions

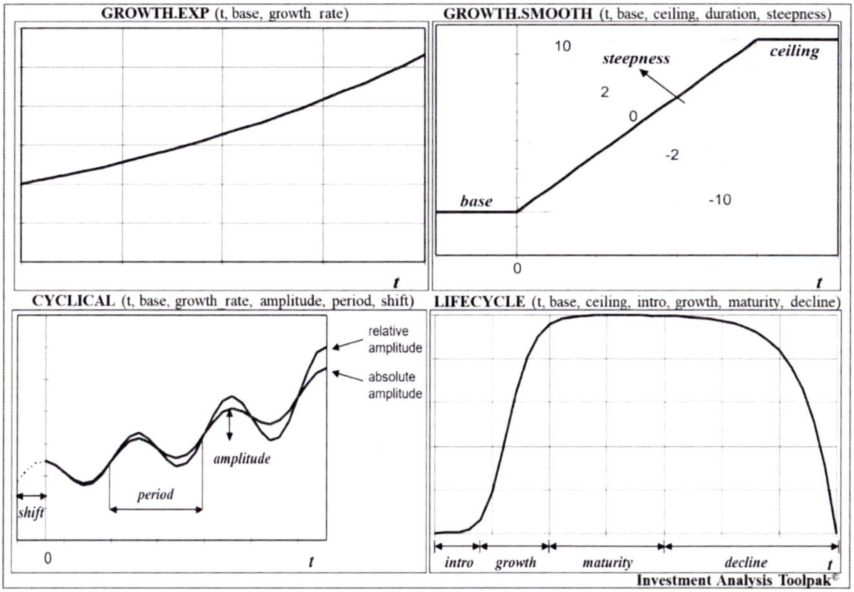

There is also a Template on which one simply selects the function and then enters the parameters that will define the growth pattern to be applied as shown in Figure 15.

Figure 15 - Growth Projections Template

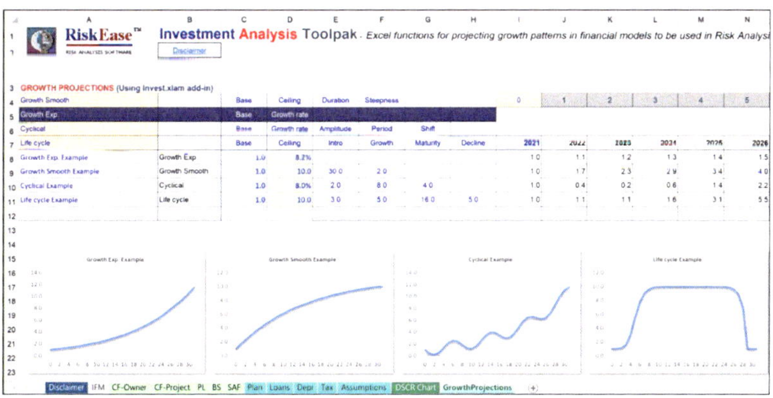

These patterns can then be applied to a cashflow projection as demonstrated in Figures 16 and 17.

Figure 16 - Projecting Growth

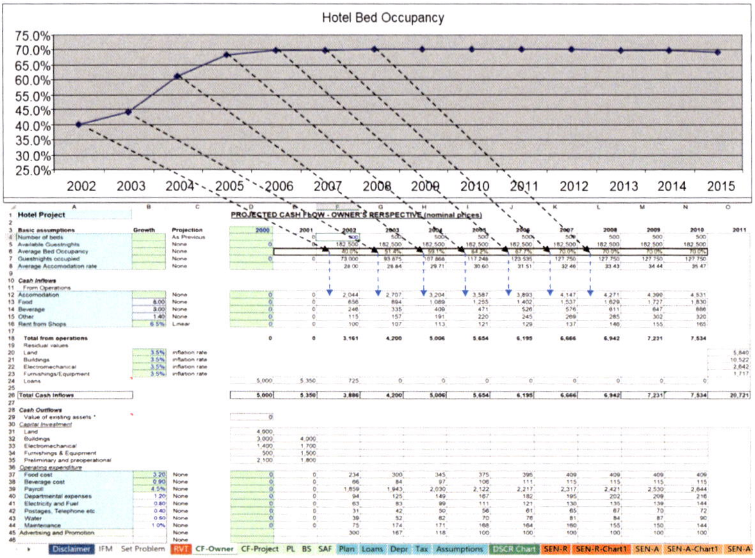

Figure 17 - Projecting Negative Growth

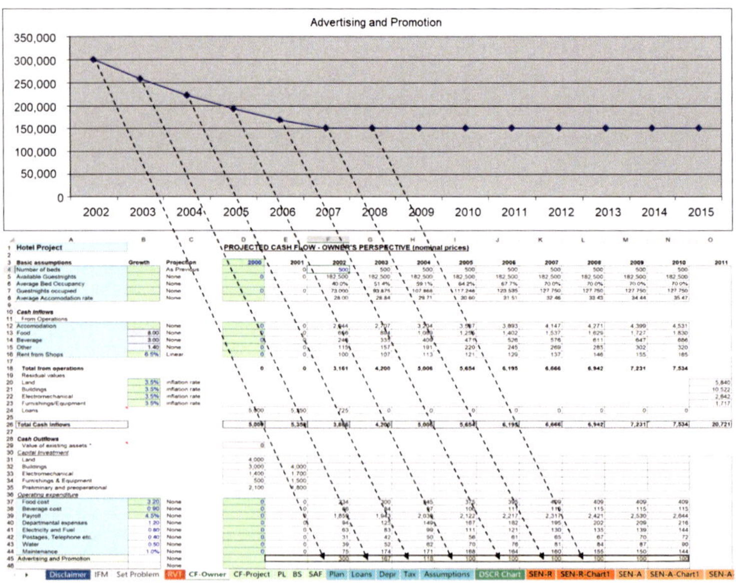

The growth patterns thus defined, and which are driven by only a few key parameters that can then be defined as risk variables in a Monte Carlo simulation can also be correlated as such through the Risk Analysis software in use where an appropriate relationship between such variables is expected to exist (such the inverse correlation between Prince and Quantity of a product). As demonstrated in Figures 18 and 19, by inversely correlating "Accommodation rates" growth rate with "Occupancy rates" ceiling.

Figure 18 - Parameters of Projected Patterns

GROWTH PROJECTIONS (Using Invest.xlam add-in)

Growth smooth	Growth projection	Base	Ceiling	Duration	Steepness		
Growth Exp.	Growth projection	Base	Growth rate				
Cyclical	Growth projection	Base	Growth rate	Amplitude	Period	Shift	
Life cycle	Growth projection	Base	Ceiling	Intro	Growth	Maturity	Decline
Occupancy	Growth Smooth	40.0%	70.0%	5	2		
Accommodation Rates	Growth Exp.	28.00	3.0%				

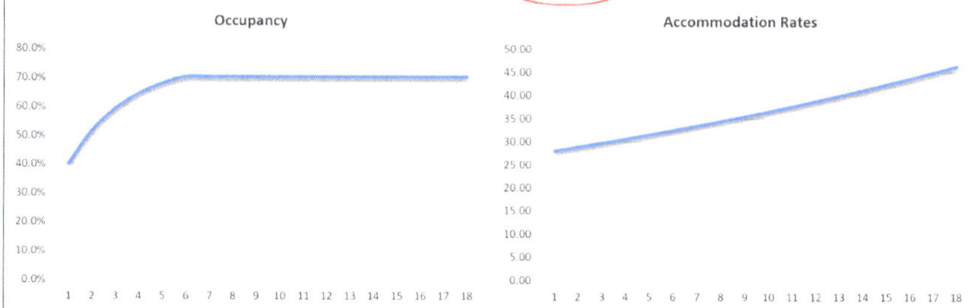

Figure 19 - Correlating parameters of growth patterns defined as risk variables

Risk Variables Table

RV No	Risk Variable Description	Base Value	Prob. Distr.	Range Min	Range Max	Parameter	Truncation Min	Truncation Max	Correlations Ind. Var.	Correlations r [-1..1]
1	Growth factor - Labour Inflator	4.50%	UNIF	3.00%	6.00%	30/70				
2	Domestic Inflation	3.50%	STEP	1.00%	5.00%	4				
3	Food Revenue per guestnight	8.00	TRNGL	5.50	10.00	44%				
4	Beverage Revenue per guestnight	3.00	TRNGL	2.00	4.50	33%				
5	Occupancy	70.0%	NORM	50.0%	85.0%	47%			RV7	-0.75
6	Occupancy - Steepness	5	NORM	3	6	47%				
7	Accommodation Rates	3.0%	NORM	0.5%	4.5%	36%				

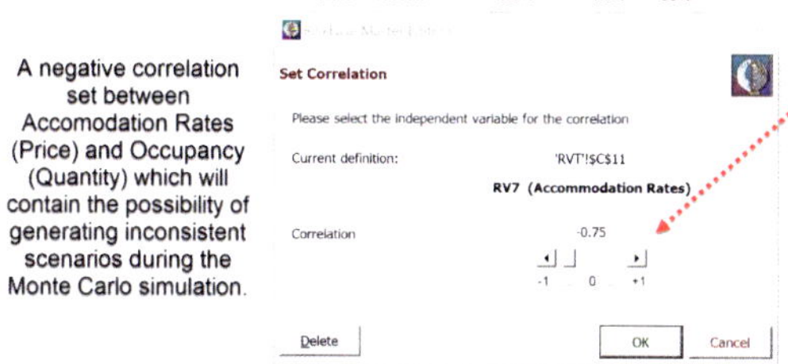

As such, the scenarios created during the simulation process will remain consistent and coherent with what may be expected to be a realistic set of circumstances. If this is left unchecked and not catered and contained in this manner it is almost certain that the Monte Carlo Simulation will not generate realistic scenarios of what may happen if the modelled business plan reflected in the cash flow projections is applied in real life.

Conclusion

Monte Carlo simulation is the only way one can attempt to gain an understanding of what to expect from a given business plan. No one can predict the future as it is, by definition, uncertain. But it is possible with prudent and comprehensive analysis to take correct decisions as they relate to capital investment. Monte Carlo can be useful if employed correctly but it can also lead one to the wrong decisions if used as a toy.

One needs first and foremost to apply the correct *cost-benefit analysis methodology* in the framework of an *integrated financial model* that projects cash flows and calculates correctly the return and debt repayment capability of the project. Secondly, it is imperative to study the *market and competitive environment* that a given project will enter. There is no substitute to real and diligent thinking that must go into the creation of a sound and valid business plan which is likely to create a sustainable competitive advantage for the intended capital investment. It is necessary but not sufficient to consider the competitive environment and identify a market performance gap that the project can exploit. It is also necessary to quantify the assumptions in the form of cash flow projections and within this framework to identify and define the *key risk variables* that drive the financial model. Hence, one should define the margins of uncertainty by setting probability distributions that capture the range and probabilities for the identified risk variables.

There is however one further issue that is often overlooked. And this pertains to how the scenarios generated during a simulation may remain realistic and relevant. Monte Carlo simulation is a mechanism that simply selects inputs from a range of multi-value probability distributions defined for the key risk variables in the financial model and records the outcome with respect to the model results that are defined (such as the return and debt service year be year). It does not automatically create consistent and realistic scenarios during a simulation. On the contrary, if left unchecked and not catered for, it will almost certainly create inconsistent and unrealistic scenarios. The Monte Carlo software employed will still generate probability distributions of the recorded outcomes from any simulation. But it will not be apparent that these may have arisen from inconsistent simulation scenarios.

State of the art Monte Carlo simulation software allow the user to *set correlation conditions* between the defined risk variables. However, this is not enough for ensuring consistency in the projections during a simulation. To achieve this, it is vital to set growth patterns with only a few parameters defined and driving the projection for some of the key risk variables. A set of typical functions that project these patterns enable the projection of such growth patterns which can then be correlated through the software by simply adding correlation coefficients to the driving parameter(s) of the defined functions (such as the *ceiling* assumed or the *growth rate* or even the *duration*).

To summarise, for a thoughtful assessment of risk in capital investment decisions on needs:

1. To understand and apply in the form of an integrated financial model the correct Cost-Benefit analysis methodology.
2. To analyse the market that the project will enter and compete in is and to prudently study it arriving at an appropriate business plan.
3. To identify the key risk variables in the model and define appropriate probability distributions capable of capturing the possible range and risk associated to each.
4. To cater for correlations that may exist in the financial model and among the defined risk variables. The correlations problem has often been cited as the Achilles' heel of Monte Carlo simulation. If not catered for, it is more than likely that inconsistent and unrealistic scenarios will be arise during a probabilistic simulation. To manage and contain it, it is not enough to just correlate any two or more risk variables. It is imperative to ensure that a projected pattern remains intact and consistent during the Monte Carlo simulation process.
5. It is therefore necessary to use growth pattern functions that drive the projections with a only a few key parameters. These key parameters can then be correlated in a Monte Carlo simulation software to ensure that two correlated projected patterns in the cash flow remain consistent creating coherent and realistic scenarios during a simulation.

III. Market Analysis and Competitiveness

This chapter is based on a paper *published by Savvides, S.* as a ***Harvard Institute for International Development***, *Development Discussion Paper*, No. 755 (2000)

The next chapter highlights the need for a methodological framework on which to base projections in project appraisal applications. Following an initial definition and sizing of the relevant market of the project, the market is analysed in terms of which are the main customer groups, what their needs are, and how well existing suppliers serve these needs. The process should identify market performance gaps against which the project can position itself and develop relevant market competencies so that it can be assessed to be capable of out-performing competitors in meeting market expectations in a sustainable manner. This should be the essence of any project appraisal. The analyst should seek to find those elements of competitiveness that are likely to make the project a successful enterprise in its market. The quantification part of this exercise should lead to the modelling and compilation of the cash flow projections. The projected numbers should reflect the competitive analysis.

Introduction

When a project is being appraised, a set of quantitative assumptions are compiled in the form of a cash flow model which is supposed to reflect the outcome of the proposed capital investment and the impact it is likely to have in its environment. It is quite easy to assert that the project products will sell at prices that grow at constant rates every year or that the volume of sales will be increasing at two percent a year or that operating costs will be increasing at the expected rate of inflation and so on. Who can argue with the wisdom of a simple projection and indeed what can you put in its place? The fact is that the projected cash flow model must be fed with numerical data that must be furnished one way or another. Whether one spends ten days or two minutes in arriving at a number to be used in the appraisal, it is still no more than just another number in the projections. It is not suggested that analysts do not take due care to gather the "correct information" but rather that there is always a high degree of residual uncertainty in any attempt to forecast the future. Indeed, the likelihood of a project unfolding in real life the way it was modelled and in the specified quantities as projected in the cost-benefit analysis evaluation is infinitely small[4].

There are commonly two problems with projecting data. The first is, that no matter how much one researches and thinks through an estimate one is still forced to reduce it down to a single number. This, by itself, means that the projected number is assigned 100% probability of occurrence. When looking into the future we cannot project anything as certain. We can however assign probabilities of occurrence to various outcomes but that would mean that a single cash flow projection would not suffice. Even by allowing the values of only a small number of variables to vary there are thousands of possible combinations of probabilities each generating different cash flow scenarios. To this end, risk analysis based on the Monte-Carlo simulation technique has come to the rescue and is increasingly being made use of in project appraisal applications[5].

The second problem involves the actual data gathered and how it is modelled. To make an accurate projection, one must be able to understand what are the key success factors of an economic enterprise (be it in the public or private sector), employ a conceptual model or framework that takes these factors into consideration and test whether the project as designed is able to compete successfully in its market environment. The way project appraisal has generally been conducted suggests that project analysts are not too concerned with such questions as what makes a successful business and whether the project has what it takes to compete in its market. In the experience of the author, this attitude hides a lack of skills, which is the major cause of project evaluation failures.

Looking at the problem from a practical perspective, the question is how it would be possible to improve the analysis without having to subject the analyst to tedious business school type of training or without having to commission specific market research for each appraisal project. Indeed, would any of these options guarantee a solution to the problem? Although marketing background and professional market research can be helpful, they

---

[4] In a post-research study of 1015 World Bank projects, it was found that the projected results were grossly off-target. See Pohl Gerhard and Mihaljek Dubravko, "Project Evaluation and Uncertainty in Practice." The World Bank Economic Review, Volume 6, Number 2, pages 255-277, May 1992).

[5] The author has developed "RiskMaster" a risk analysis software program that allows the application of the Monte-Carlo Simulation technique on spreadsheet models. See Savvakis C. Savvides, "Risk Analysis in Investment Appraisal", Project Appraisal Vol. 9, 1, pages 3-18, March 1994. Beech Tree Publishing.

are neither necessary nor sufficient to ensure a thoughtful market analysis in project evaluation. In most cases it will be like crushing a walnut with a hammer. What is needed is awareness of the market framework in which a project will operate and an ability to use common sense to gather and analyse the available market data.

The market and competitive analysis framework

Figure 20 - The Competitive Environment of a Project

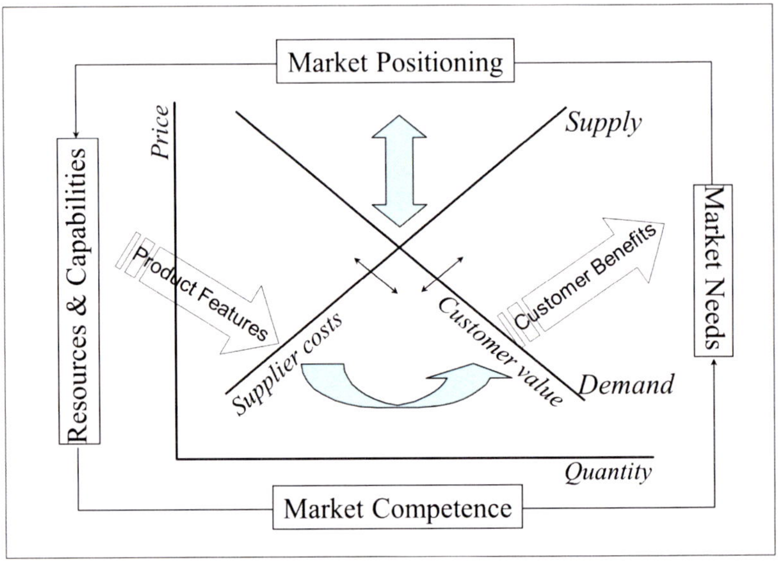

The market and competitive analysis framework, as illustrated in Figure 20, is offered as a conceptual background by which to gather, analyse and interpret data about the project and its market. The core of the model is the project's market. Competitiveness revolves around the interactions of suppliers and consumers in the market. Suppliers compete in a market by using available resources to serve market needs better than their competitors. Their offerings take the form of product features designed to generate customer benefits that meet customer needs. To the extent that existing competitors fail to meet market expectations they leave behind market performance gaps. For a new project to be successful, therefore, it must identify unsatisfied market needs for which it can develop competencies and position itself to fill market performance gaps. Project competitiveness is assumed to be a factor of the ability of the project to develop *market competencies* and to correctly *position* itself in the market as part of a continuing self-correcting process.

The project's market

Projects exist and operate within markets. To pose and attempt to answer the project competitiveness question it is imperative to first define the project relevant market and disaggregate both the demand and supply into its basic component parts.

The essence of a market is epitomised by the act of exchange. People strive to improve their quality of life by seeking to acquire (consume) products and services that are perceived to be capable of satisfying their needs. To achieve this, they enter into exchange agreements with other people (suppliers) who likewise have their need profiles and economic assets (or capabilities) so that through the act of exchange (be it labour services in return for a wage or tomatoes for potatoes) both parties consider themselves better off. Economic value is nothing more than the net benefit (or utility) generated through exchange. An economy based on free market exchange, by and large, directs economic resources into their most productive uses as each economic unit strives to maximise its own welfare by producing those goods that it can market *efficiently* from a spectrum of products that other *people want most*.

The value at which a product is sold (or price) and the amount of it being exchanged in a market situation results from the demand and supply profiles of consumers and suppliers. Micro-economic theory is based on a conceptual model, which however, assumes the existence of a homogeneous product, perfect knowledge, and perfect accessibility to the marketplace. Moreover, micro-economic theory identifies that demand and supply, can change as a result of a number of factors, which except for the price of the product, are usually assumed to remain constant during the period of analysis. A change in any of these factors represents a shift (left or right) in the position of the demand or supply curve. The demand and supply functions of a micro-economic model is illustrated in Figure 21:

Figure 21 - The economic determinants of demand and supply

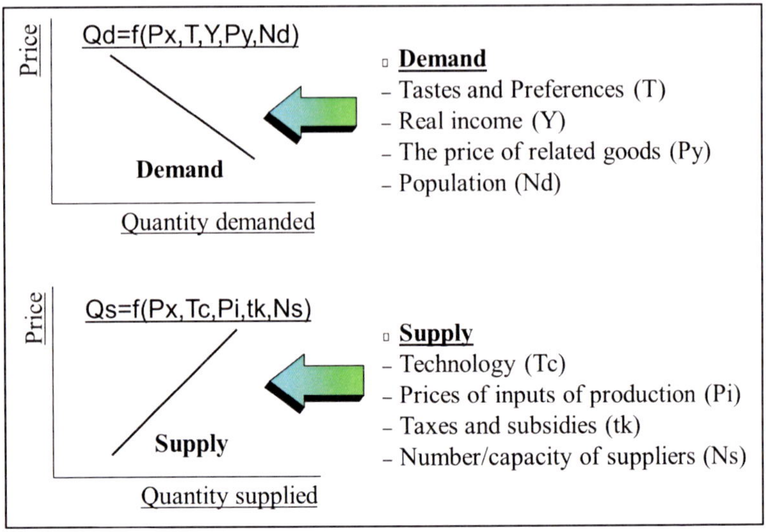

Market volume (the quantity consumed in a certain period) and market value (the money value of the transactions in a period) can be measured at the equilibrium point where "Demand" meets "Supply"[6] as illustrated in Figures 22 and 23:

[6] The existence of monopolistic power or the ability of firms to differentiate their products may cause the price to be higher and quantity lower than the equilibrium point under conditions of perfect competition.

Figure 22 - The market demand and supply

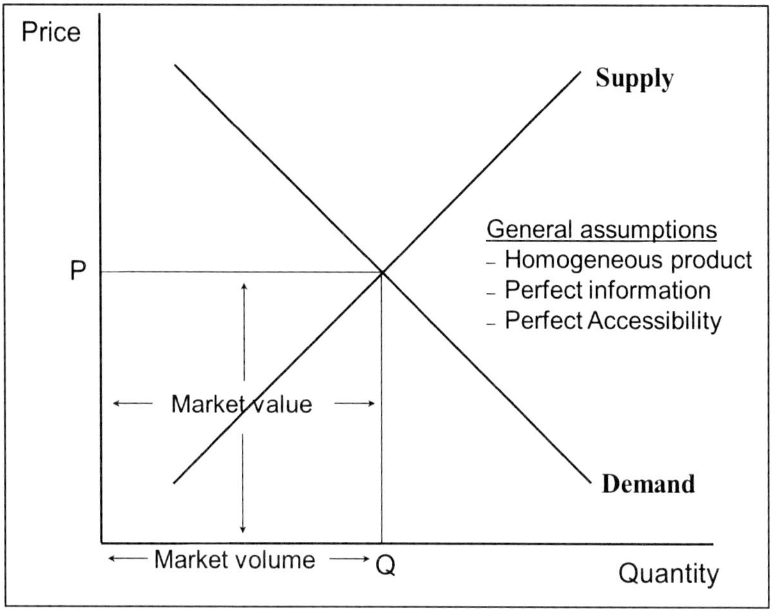

A market demand and supply curve are an aggregate of the individual demand and supply functions of each consumer and supplier participating in that market. As illustrated in the diagram below, the market demand and supply curve are the horizontal summation of the demand and supply curves of each consumer and supplier respectively.

Figure 23 - Market is the adding up of the individual Demand and Supply curves

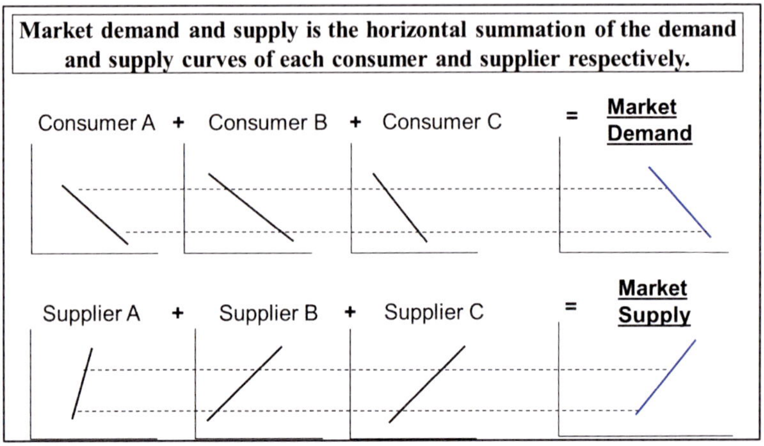

A market therefore is made up of many individual consumers and suppliers where each consumer has a different demand function, and each supplier has a different supply function. The search of a project's competitiveness begins from this basic fact. Since, all consumers and suppliers are different then there must be more than one way for a project to attain and sustain a competitive position. But it would surely be a daunting task to attempt to find an optimum competitive strategy, even if it was ever possible to gather all the necessary information to define each individual demand and supply function. But fortunately, although everybody is different many market participants have typically similar demand and supply profiles. And it is not by chance that this is so. For example, two persons of the same sex, age and social background who are exposed to similar stimuli (school, family, values, etc.) are likely to want similar things and have similar market behaviour. There may of course exist differences in personalities, but there again, one can identify and categorise types of people to some basic character traits (the aggressive, the revolutionary, the conservative, the fashion follower, and so on). Hence, while everybody is different, it is usually possible with some basic market research to understand and describe the types of customer groups (market segments) that make up the market.

The determinant factors of demand and supply together with the tools of market segmentation provide the keys to finding a competitive marketing strategy for the project. To understand demand, one should define the behaviour of the typical market segments making up the demand of a product with respect to each segment's responsiveness to price movements, aspects of quality (tastes and preferences) and, where relevant, changes in income. On the supply side, competitors should be compared according to their ability to reduce costs and add features (through technology, efficient use of inputs of production and creativity) so that customer value is maximised.

Marketing is sometimes defined as the art of creating loyal customers. A new project should identify its potential customers and justify why it can win them over from the competition. Out of the many project scenarios that are possible from varying the elements of a market offering there are a number which, given the capabilities of the project, have the potential for making the project a competitive one. But first, one should define and size-up the market that is immediately relevant to the project.

Defining the project relevant market

The need to define a market usually determines the type of definition selected. As Day, Shocker and Srivastava (1979) point out:

> "Ultimately all product-market definitions are arbitrary. They exist because of recurring needs to comprehend market structures and impose some order on complex market environments. But this situation could not be otherwise. One reason is the wide variety of decision contexts which dictate different definitions of boundaries".

A market, as defined in this paper, is conceptually different from the commonly used term of an industry. While an industry refers to products with similar physical and technical characteristics, a market refers to products that serve the same basic market need. The boundaries of the market within which the project is expected to operate therefore depend on the degree of *substitutability* between its products and other potentially competing products. The boundaries of such definition are often difficult to establish and even harder to achieve with a high degree of consensus[7]. Within this framework, the "relevant market" is simply that part of the total potential market that is competitively accessible to the project. It is the sum of the served markets of the project and its competitors.

[7] Moran (1973) expresses the problem as follows:
"To some degree, in some circumstances, almost anything can be a partial substitute for almost anything else. A (fifteen cent) stamp substitutes to some extent for an airline ticket."

In general, the project's market should be defined in a way that permits the inclusion of all major competitors and their customers but excludes those that are only remotely related to it. A description of the project concept around the core market need becomes the starting point for the market analysis as it facilitates the identification and selection of the likely competitors and market segments of the project. In public sector projects, the perceived social need that the project is supposed to serve and the likely demand for its products or services is the very first market aspect of the project that must be researched clarified and agreed. As Jenkins and Harberger[8] point out:

> "... too often in the public sector one finds that feasibility studies have been commissioned before administrators or policy makers have a clear idea of the nature of the output and the economic and social benefits that are to be expected from it. When this occurs the terms of reference given to the consultants ... are usually so general that they are left in the awkward position of having to second-guess the government in deciding what its objectives are and what components of a potential expenditure program should be included in the project."

In defining the relevant market, the analyst should also consider whether the products of the project will be sold domestically or traded internationally. For most products sold in the international market there is usually an abundance of information from specialised journals, trade organisations and international consulting firms. However, unless the product is totally homogeneous and transport is not a major cost item, one needs to define the project relevant market as consisting of only those countries and types of customers within the countries that are accessible or cost effective to target. Markets that are evidently uneconomical to aim for should be excluded. For example, in the case of a fertiliser project in Cyprus the total world consumption of compound fertilisers for 1988 was estimated (using the supply-side market size estimate formula -see market size chapter below) at 99 million tonnes.

[8] Jenkins, Glenn P. and Harberger Arnold C. 1991 "Cost-Benefit Analysis of Investment Decisions" 2:4. Harvard Institute for International Development.

Table 2 - World Market for Compound Fertilisers

Supply Side World Market Estimate - example

Supply and Demand for Compound Fertilisers

(million tonnes) - 1988

	Production	Imports	Exports	Consumption
West Europe	30.5	5.8	-7.6	28.7
East Europe	16.1	0.2	-1.1	15.2
Africa	1.9	0.9	-0.2	2.6
North America	29.1	0.3	-0.4	29.0
Latin America	10.0	0.6	-0.1	10.5
Asia/Oceania	11.6	2.3	-0.9	13.0
Total world market	99.2	10.1	-10.3	99.0

Source: Fertecon

Was this, however, the relevant market for the project under review? After commissioning a specialised consulting organisation in London to help the team of analysts define the market for the project it was soon realised that the Cyprus project could only consider a very small part of the total international market as accessible or cost effective to aim for.

Table 3 - The Project Relevant Market

Relevant Market for Cyprus Project Estimate - example

Consumption of Compound Fertilisers

(million tonnes) - 1988

	Consumption
France	6.80
Italy	2.40
Spain	2.40
Greece	1.20
Saudi Arabia	0.20
Libya	0.20
Local Market	0.04
Relevant market	13.24

Source: Fertecon

The Cyprus fertiliser plant could only sell to countries in Western Europe, which were still using a particular type of compound fertiliser that Cyprus was able to produce and could deliver in relatively small batches. The size and growth prospect of the sub-market that was relevant to the Cyprus project was very different, and far smaller, than the total world fertiliser market. While the total world market for 1988 was estimated at about 99 million tonnes, the project relevant market was only 13 million tonnes. The relevant market included only the consumption of countries that were competitively accessible by the project, taking into consideration factors such as distance and the capacity of the Cyprus project to serve these markets, given its scale, production capabilities and the opportunities available to transport fertiliser shipments in the required frequency to these countries.

Figure 24 - Levels of Market Definition

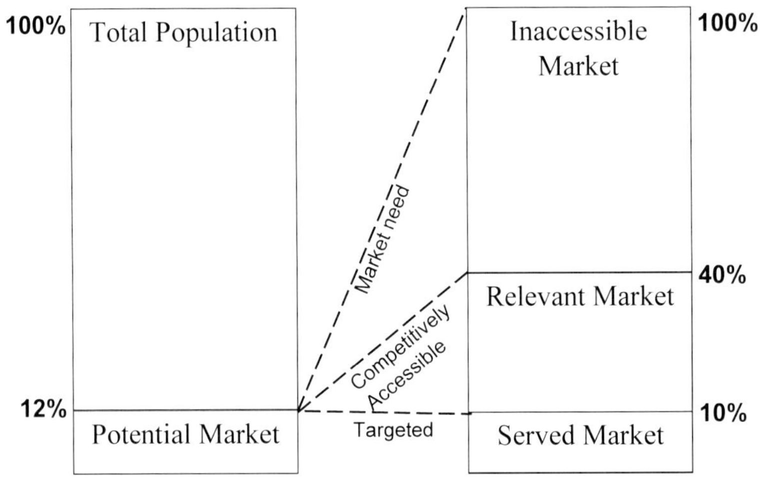

Estimating market size

Market size refers to the volume and value of the products or services consumed, or expected to be consumed, in a period. There are two ways one can go about estimating market size: supply-side and demand-side measures. In supply-side estimates, volume and value are measured from the point of view of production and trade intermediaries. In demand-side estimates, market size is derived from studying the behaviour of the consumers in the marketplace.

To arrive at a *supply-side market size estimate*[9] for a given period based on official published statistics for a country one should apply the following formula[10]:

$$Ms = P + (I - E) + (So - Sc)$$

Where: Ms= Market size (Supply side definition)
P = Production of relevant products
I = Imports of relevant products
E = Exports of relevant products
So= Opening stocks
Sc= Closing stocks[11]

To arrive at the *demand-side market size estimate* one should apply the following formula:

$$Md = n\ q\ p$$

Where: Md= Market size (Demand side definition)
n = penetration (number of customers)
q = total volume purchased per customer in period12
p = average price paid

The demand-side market estimate is very helpful especially in situations where information is not readily available. The formula can easily be applied with only some basic population statistics, such as the number of households, and a few survey questions to establish likely patterns of consumption among various groups of the population.

---

[9] For an example of a supply size estimate of market size see the Compound Fertilizers calculation in the previous section.

[10] Value statistics are published based on ex-works, wholesale, F.O.B. or C.I.F. prices (not retail prices). To arrive at the total value of the market one must add the profit margins of the intermediaries involved in the delivery of the product to the consumer and taxes/duties.

[11] (So - Sc) can be assumed away if the market is stable. It can be estimated based on the percentage level of opening and closing stocks that major suppliers keep. This information is usually available from the companies' published accounts of recent years.

[12] Purchase quantity per customer (q) in a period can be the product of:

$$q = f\ a$$

where: f = Frequency (number of purchases in a year)
a = Amount purchased (average quantity purchased)

Projecting growth

There are various growth trends one can use to project market size variables. By gathering enough historical data it is usually possible to fit a growth line. A linear projection, however, is not always the most suitable way to model growth patterns for market variables. For example, market share projections lend themselves to better modelling through the employment of exponential growth rates while prices of international marketed commodity goods may follow cyclical or even erratic paths. The diagram below demonstrates some growth patterns that can be used in project appraisal projections[13]:

Figure 25 - Projecting Growth

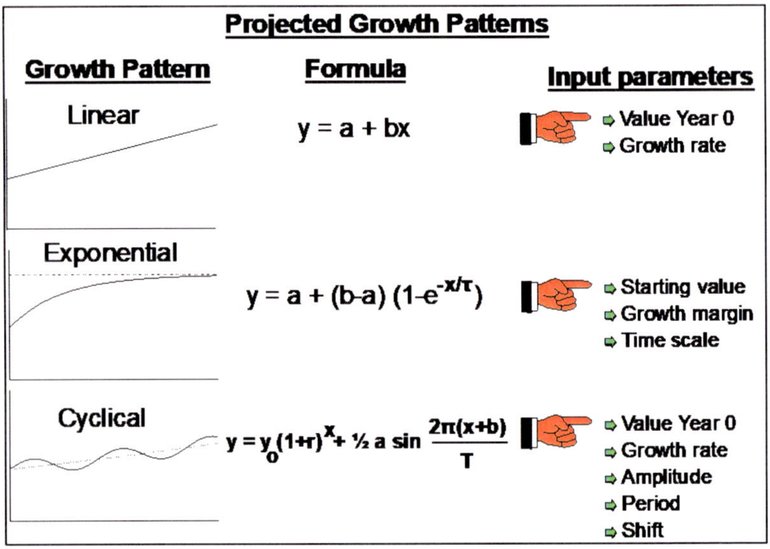

Historical data alone are, quite often, not a sufficient base for forecasting the future development of the market. The analyst must also look to the

[13] The examples displayed are some of the functions included in the "Investment Analysis Toolpak" by RiskEase Ltd. This is a software module included with "RiskEase Master Edition" whereby a set of Microsoft Excel functions are provided to enable the coherent projection of various growth patterns like *exponential growth*, *smooth growth*, *life cycle* and *cyclical*. These are useful in investment appraisal applications but moreover enable the rational projections to use in risk analysis using Monte Carlo Simulation. For example, providing just five parameters can define the "CYCLICAL" function (base, growth rate, amplitude, period and shift) can easily define and drive a cyclical projection.

future by reviewing the current state and the expected changes in the determinant factors of demand and supply. Market forecasts should reflect how factors like income, tastes, technology, and prices of related products might affect the development of the market during the life of the project.

Figure 26 - Market Growth and Equilibrium

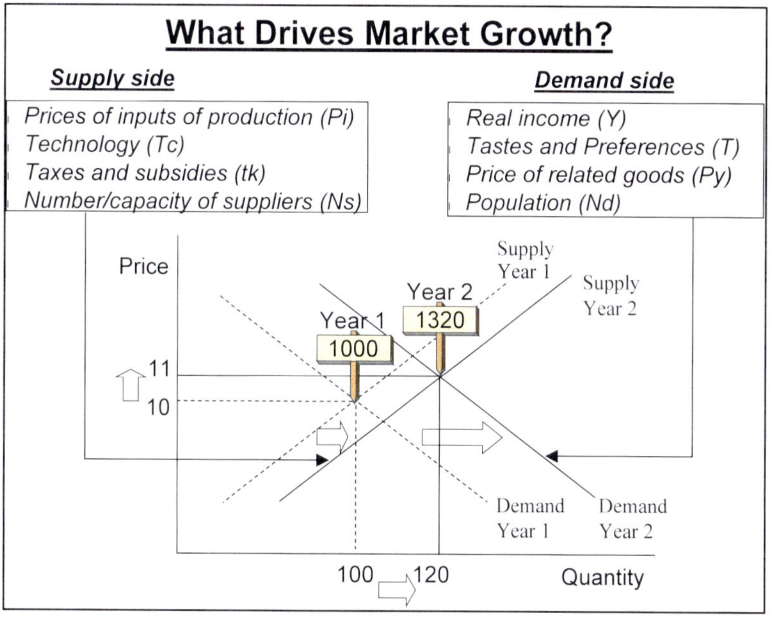

A change in any of these factors causes a shift in the demand and supply curve. A shift in demand or supply initially brings the market into a transitional disequilibrium phase and, subsequently into equilibrium whereby a new price and quantity relationship is established.

Some markets may be at a stage of almost perpetual disequilibrium. For example, the market for personal computers, propelled by advances in technology and acute competition between many suppliers (who have access to the technology) as well as the ever-increasing higher standard of living (and better education) of the population base, is almost constantly keeping the market equilibrium in a state of flux and this is expected to be so for some years to come. In the fertilisers market, the introduction of huge supplies from Morocco in the late eighties was expected to have the market at disequilibrium, pushing prices down, for many years.

In assessing market growth, the analyst must consider whether the market is at an equilibrium stage and to what extent possible changes in any of the determinant factors (including the introduction of the project itself) are likely to affect the projected price and quantity through their impact on demand and supply. Sometimes, a market that is going through a long disequilibrium stage is easier to predict. The factors causing the turbulence can be identified and at least the direction of the projections in the first, but in present value terms most important years would be correct. A market, on the other hand, which is at a stage of relative equilibrium, where the many market forces affecting price and quantity cannot be easily assessed, poses a bigger problem. A growth rate error of a single percentage point can sometimes make the difference between a viable and non-viable project! So, is this the Achilles heel of project appraisal? How can anyone forecast accurately with so many uncertain variables affecting quantity and price?

The author believes that there can be no correct answer. There are some things, however, an analyst should bear in mind. Sophistication and complexity do not always lead to better predictions. The more sophistication you put in, the better modelling you need to take care of the many relationships of the variables you use and to arrive at the weights of importance to be attached to each parameter. Econometric modelling is one attempt to use economic theory to specify the relationships and arrive at a prediction based on forecasts of such variables. Even when this is possible however, econometric modelling suffers from one basic deficiency. It relies heavily on past data to forecast the future. To give an example, take the case of an econometric study that aimed at forecasting tourist arrivals in Cyprus. The historical fact that increases in the level of income in the source countries (GDP) was a reliable predictor of tourist arrivals in the 70s and 80s, when there was a shortage of supply of beds is, according to some critics, of little relevance to the current situation. Common sense would suggest that the competitiveness of Cyprus as a Mediterranean tourist destination has been eroded because of many other factors such as the deterioration of quality of service, the strong local currency and the restrictions and constraints imposed on European tour operators through the monopolistic practices of the national airline. These factors are either qualitative in nature or not historical enough to be used in an econometric forecast.

A sounder advice for the project analyst would be to keep the prediction simple but relevant to the logical conclusion to be derived from a thoughtful assessment of both the historical facts gathered and any expected changes in the determinant factors during the life of the project. One should try not to fall into the trap of fitting lines to historical data and thinking that because of mathematical sophistication alone one will end up with a more accurate prediction. If it were that simple to predict the future, there would not be a need to take a risk about anything. The fact that historical data may suggest some trend or pattern does not mean that extending it into the future would predict well. Take for example the prices of internationally traded goods (e.g., mineral products and commodities) that generally exhibit cyclical fluctuations. The cycle size is never the same and the risk of ignoring the fact that there is almost equal probability for the projected prices to follow a downward rather than an upward path can be devastating to the project. To give an example, in appraising a project regarding a chemical factory producing fertilisers, after studying historical data, the analysts fitted and projected a cyclical pattern of international prices. They only got one thing wrong. Instead of the starting year of the project being on an upturn, it was in fact on a downturn. As a result, a few years after implementation the plant ran into liquidity problems and closed.

The problem is that any single projection has only an infinitesimally small chance of being accurate, while the impact of even a very small error in the prices or quantities projected can be tremendous. The disaggregation of an identified pattern into its basic parameters can therefore be useful only within the context of risk analysis. Historical data can be analysed to determine the potential variability of the underlying parameters of a pattern to be projected. Consider the following example that illustrates how historical data may be used to derive probability distributions that can be used in a Monte-Carlo simulation type of risk analysis:

The observed data displayed in the example above show some cyclical pattern (smoothed by the continuous cyclical line in Figure 27).

Growth rate: The growth rate of a line of best fit for the projected period (indicated by the dotted line in the graph).

Cycle Period: The time duration of a cycle.

Amplitude: The distance between the highest and lowest point of a cycle.

A shift factor: The point of the cycle period that is assigned to the first-year value. This factor determines whether the first years of the project will be on an up-turn or a down-turn trend.

Figure 27 - Cyclical growth pattern projection

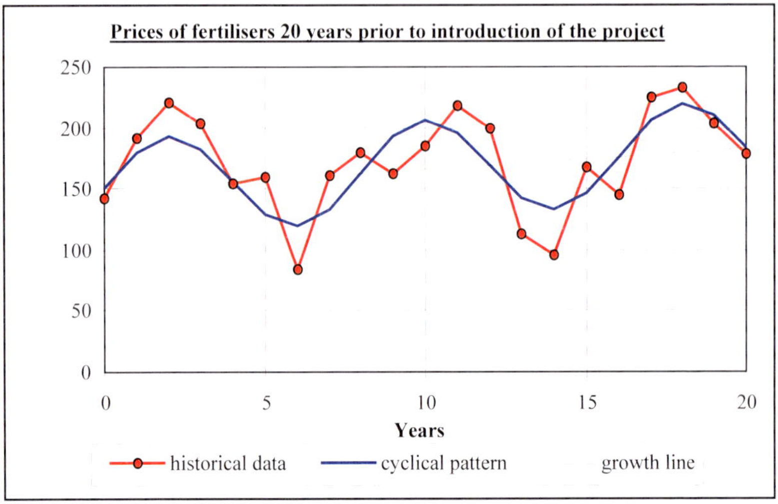

These four parameters and possibly an additional random error factor can define a realistic cyclical path that can be used to project fertilizer prices over the project horizon, which in this example is ten years. By plotting a regression line for all sets of consecutive ten-year periods contained in the data it is possible to derive frequency distributions of the values possible for the "growth rate" variable which can then be converted to a probability distribution to be used in a risk analysis application. Similarly, probability distributions can be derived for the other parameters in the cyclical function. For example, the possible cycle periods (e.g., 3-8 years) or the amplitude of a cycle (e.g.,100-240) can be plotted in frequency distributions such as the one displayed below:

It is also possible to observe whether any correlations exist between the parameters. For example, it may be more realistic to correlate positively the "cycle period" values to the "amplitude" values generated during a simulation run. That is to say that the distance from a low to a high point in a cycle is likely to be greater if the period of the cycle is longer.[14]

[14] The limits and weights of the probability distribution derived through this method should be extended somewhat to allow for the possibility of a future value being higher or lower than any historical record at hand and to take account of any expert information regarding expectations about the future.

The result of a projection that is based on probability distributions as inputs is a probability distribution of the outcome (or its expected value and standard deviation). Through this process it is therefore possible to project growth and calculate the impact of the inherent variability of the parameters of a market growth function. The steps for projecting market growth patterns, using a Monte Carlo simulation program, are as follows:

- Identify the parameters of a function that can plot the pattern in the data
- Analyse the data to set the limits of possible variability for each parameter and derive frequency distributions; convert these to probability distributions
- Set correlation conditions where necessary and
- Through a process of simulation by appropriate software arrive at a probability distribution of the expected outcome.[15]

The impact of market structure

Figure 28 - Market structure and competitive forces

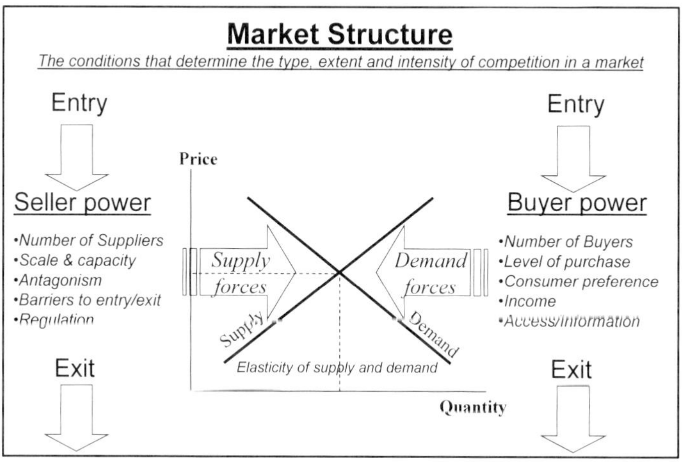

Market structure refers to the composition of the market, the relative power of suppliers in relation to customers and the intensity of competition. Is the market composed of many small suppliers with basically homogeneous

---

[15] RiskEase© by RiskEase Ltd is one such software package that can be used to apply risk analysis to Excel spreadsheet model. It also includes the "Investment analysis toolpak" which is a set of pre-defined Excel functions with which one can project growth patterns that are common in investment appraisal financial models.

products having little influence over price or is it composed of only a few major companies with differentiated products and a high degree of leverage in the market? Is the market regulated, subsidised, or over-taxed? What is the level of antagonism or collusion within the market? How easy and costly is it to enter or exit the market? These are the types of questions one need to answer to assess the impact of market structure on the project and vice-versa.

To illustrate how market structure factors, affect the relationship of supply intermediaries in a market consider the following example of the market for holiday packages in Western Europe in the 1980s and early 1990s.

Figure 29 - The Value chain and competitive power

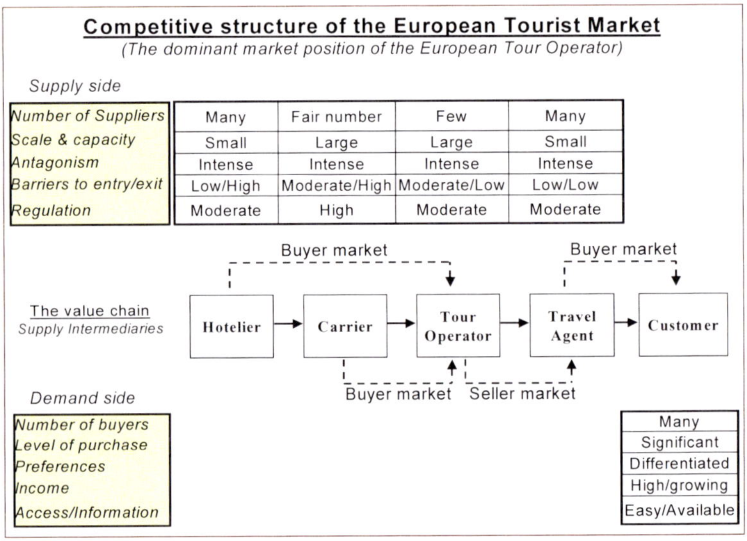

Big tour operators in Europe have been able to drive the market for holiday packages for more than twenty years. Following a period of mergers and take-overs in the source countries (notably Germany and the UK) a handful of tour operating companies reached a scale and level of know-how that afforded them a commanding market position. Their market dominance was driven, by the massive scale of their operations, and the bargaining power that this generates, coupled with their ability to apply marketing techniques to package the product so that the customer is satisfied. Moreover, major tour operating firms have been taking full advantage of the fragmented nature of the highly competitive supplier markets.

The "carrier" market, which consists of a fair number of airlines with an undifferentiated product, was hardly able to dictate its terms. Most airlines in Europe were national companies that were by and large shielded from competition. In the late 1980s because of the impending liberalisation of the airline market, many airlines found themselves in a survival struggle with their governments unable or unwilling to help. As the most critical factor for profitability in this market is aircraft occupancy, most of the airlines were only too happy to let go of their spare capacity to tour operators at marginal cost pricing or to charter out their aircraft to tour operating companies.

In the "tourist accommodation" market, the tour operators were once again in a commanding position because on the customer side there was not a great demand for a differentiated product and on the suppliers' side the product very rarely amounted to much more than having the location and the room available.

The third intermediaries, the travel agents, depended almost totally on the tour operators to provide them with competitive packages. They were simply a distribution channel, or resellers, for the tour operators to deliver their products to their customers. They added little value to the final product for the customer. The marketing mix, including the pricing, was being pretty much determined on a large scale by the tour operator companies who were creating the holiday packages offered through the travel agent. Hence, the tour operator being sufficiently big and armed with only his marketing skills has managed to become the supplier of the tourist product, relegating all the other suppliers to mere inputs.

In recent years, tour operators have been observed to invest some of their profits in gaining "shelf space" with travel agents and in acquiring equity share in strategic hotel accommodation units. Some of them, with varying success, have also invested in the airline business. This current move of the tour operators towards acquiring some of the inputs of their product is to some extent transforming the market realities. There are four market forces that seem to drive the tour operator towards a vertical integration policy and a dramatic re-examination of his role.

- The customer is increasingly becoming more demanding (quality conscious) with the tour operator seeking new ways to satisfy this need.

- The competition among tour operators, exacerbated by the very fact that "other competitors are moving into their supplier markets" intensifies the quest for suitable acquisition targets, alliances and joint ventures.
- An over-supply of tourist beds and available air travel seats prompted hotel owners, airlines and tour operators to offer occasional special offers in the summer period. The market has reacted by learning the benefits of reserving a holiday package late. The phenomenon of late bookings is now a serious concern to the major tour operators because it allows competition from smaller tour operators and even travel agencies. The customer habit of studying the tour operator brochures and planning his vacation three to six months before is now changing.
- Buyer behaviour is expected to change even more rapidly with the introduction of information technology both at the travel agent level and in the home. By the year 2000 most homes in the developed world will be able to plan and book their holidays at home through browsing the Internet on their personal computer.

Within the above context, it becomes increasingly good business logic for tour operators to seek suitable partners to secure the competencies that are likely to shape the successful "tourist product" supplier of the 21st century. The competitive organisation of the future will emerge as the one that can anticipate the position of the various players before the dust of the current restructuring of the market settles.

Understanding market expectations

"Necessity is the mother of invention". In a modern society the maxim still holds true; only instead of inventing to satisfy one's own needs, in the marketplace, suppliers invent to satisfy the needs of their customers. Those suppliers who understand the needs of their customers better than others and manage to develop appropriate skills and products are the successful ones. Hence, the first point of reference of any business should not be what the competition is doing but rather how to best serve the needs of their customers.

But needs vary by many factors; the situation of the consumer, his income and wealth, the people that influence his life, his level of education and ambitions, and so on and so forth. Current management thinking does not pay enough attention to the importance of needs perhaps because it is very hard to understand and to draw general conclusions from, particularly because they change almost constantly. Yet, this is exactly where the key to business success lies. It is therefore imperative that to be competitive, one should adopt systems by which it is possible to closely monitor customer needs, learn the appropriate skills and technologies and respond accordingly in a quick and efficient manner. At any given point in time the competitive organisation should be aware of the current market expectations regarding the market needs which its business mission is to serve.

The need to go beyond the identification of customer needs and to genuinely try and understand their pulse, aspirations and the extent of their imagination cannot be over-stated. Schnedler (1996), following market research by which Hewlett-Packard, using an approach, which they term "strategic market modelling" whereby they derived a customer-needs based segmentation and perceptions about competitors, concludes as follows:

> *"[Through] needs-based segmentation and modelling [we were able to] define customer segments by "what the customer needs". Knowing customer' needs is [however] not enough. To have what we call a truly imaginative understanding of user needs, we must know the customers so well that we fully comprehend both their spoken and unspoken needs - now and in the future. We need to know what new products, features and services will surprise and delight them. We need to understand their world so well that we can bring new technology to problems that customers may not yet truly realise they have. Our ultimate goal is this deeper, richer level of understanding."*

The term "market expectations" refers to this deeper understanding of the customer and his expectations. It means anticipating what may make him happy even before he is able to realise it himself. "Market expectations" is therefore more than just a reference to the notional *ideal* product for a market segment. It means thinking and feeling like the consumer. The depth of market enquiry may thus be more important in understanding real needs than the spread of market research. In other words, it may be more useful getting under the skin of a single consumer rather than asking a thousand to respond to a series of descriptive questions. Of course, once you touch upon a real customer need you may form a hypothesis and test its validity through more extensive market research. Business history has many examples of entrepreneurs who conceived great product ideas without ever conducting market research. They managed to do that just by studying people and being able to put themselves in their place in a genuine effort to truly understand their expectations, aspirations and fears.

Common versus distinctive needs

Consumers do not understand technology or even products. They can only appreciate what products can do for them. As Levitt (1960) points out "people actually do not buy gasoline… what they buy is the right to continue driving their cars." The only thing people understand is their needs. They use their imagination and the resources available to them to find ways to best satisfy these needs.

In defining the limits of the relevant market, one seeks to identify common market needs that are shared by all consumers; these are used to identify potential customer groups and to size up the market (demand-side market definition). Common market needs may also serve as close approximations to the determinant choice factors by which products are perceptually positioned in the market (see "market positioning" below). But while all consumers making up market demand share the same broad market need, they are also distinctly different by way of what customer benefits they seek and in how they try to fulfil those needs. It is this element that makes market need based segmentation a particularly useful tool in project appraisal.

Defining market segments in terms of distinctive needs and characteristics of the main customer groups can be a powerful tool for developing an effective competitive strategy. A market-need-based segmentation should always have some implications regarding the appropriate strategy and positioning of the project. In the example below, McKinseys have used ad-hoc consumer research to arrive at the following market segmentation, which is based on distinctive motivations of holiday package users:

Figure 30 - An Example of market segmentation by distinctive expectations

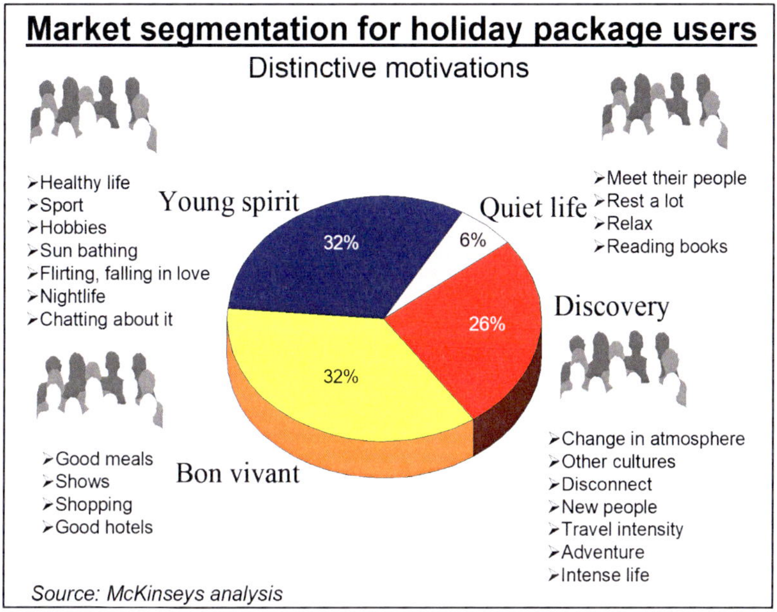

A demographic/geographic description of segments (using variables like age, income, family status, location, etc.) further enhances the usefulness of market-need based segmentation. McKinseys describe the market-need-based segments shown in the above diagram by general and distinctive demographic characteristics:

For segmentation to be useful it is necessary to gain a good understanding of customers and their needs. The importance of this point is expressed by McBurnie and Clutterbuck (1988) as follows:

> "Raw market research data will not normally provide [the necessary] understanding. If it does, the lack of refinement will make it easy for competitors to follow".

The defined market segments should be accessible, substantial in size and predictable. It is easy to select criteria that do not cluster people with similar market needs together or are so complex that make the defined market segments inaccessible and operationally useless. For example, it is increasingly being discovered by tourism organisations that, although grouping tourists on geographical or national criteria is a neat way of aggregating the tourism market (leaving no gaps or double counting), it inevitably leads towards market segments whose members have little in common in terms of predictable market behaviour. Such segmentation is therefore of little use for the development of competitive strategy. As illustrated in the McKinseys' example, recent efforts to analyse the European tourist market go beyond national borders emphasising the motivations, the personal and situational characteristics of typical groups of consumers across Western Europe.

Figure 31 - Distinctive characteristics segmentation

Example of distinctive characteristics of different market segments of European consumers of holiday packages (users)

Characteristics / Segments	Young Spirit	Bon Vivant	Discovery	Quiet life
Destination	Islands	Cultural Europe	Sunny Europe/North Africa	Close resorts
Activity	Same place	Circuit	Some excursion	Same place
Information	Friends	Image of the place	Brochures	Friends and relatives, previous visits
Company	Group of friends	Wife/husband Girlfriend/boyfriend	Group of friends	Family, alone
Age	16-30	46-65	31-45	31-45
Job	Student	Business-man	Worker, professional	Employee, professional
Transport	Charter	Coach	Scheduled	Charter

Source: McKinseys analysis

Factors that determine consumer choice usually fall into two broad categories: quality and price. Although price is conceptually straightforward in all markets (it is always important to get the lowest price possible for a given product[16]), "quality" can have various dimensions and manifestations. It is not enough to assert that a project will provide products of high quality. In every market, quality is defined in terms of the fundamental market needs that a product aims to satisfy. In the summer holiday package market for example, although there are many distinctive benefits that various segments

[16] There are a few rare exceptions to this general rule. For example, in some cases where the price is taken to be an indication of quality, such as in the case of some table wines, a very low price may discourage a prospective consumer.

seek to have, it may be possible to reduce the basic market needs to a short list such as:

- Suitable sun and sea location
- Comfortable staying conditions
- Entertainment/fun
- Affordability/Price

Market needs represent the basic determinants of consumer choice[17]. They are the dimensions in which consumers perceive and position the various products in the market. Each market segment attaches a different level of importance to each of the basic market needs characterising the relevant market thereby giving rise to different "consumer need profiles".

Identifying market performance gaps

Market performance gaps refer to the notional distance between market expectations and the level of satisfaction (or customer value) attained by the products and services of current suppliers. A market performance gap applies both to the reasonable expectations of existing as well as potential customers. To give an example, consider the case of ice cream consumption in Cyprus. The import of ice-cream products as well as the basic raw materials (milk powder and flavours) was restricted up until the end of 1995. Following the signing of the GATT agreement the market was flooded with imported ice-cream products. The prices were sometimes 100% more expensive than before. Yet consumption, as well as overall customer satisfaction was more than doubled. Before 1995, the Government of Cyprus kept refusing to give licences to import ice-cream products arguing that there is over capacity locally and that therefore the market is fully served. The only thing that such a policy achieved was to severely limit the capacity of local producers to satisfy the market. With import restrictions in place, local producers faced a secured market which however, because of a huge performance gap was in fact less than half in volume and even significantly less in value than what it could potentially have been if it was properly catered for. The very government intervention that limited competition, and provided them protection, was in fact the reason why the local suppliers could not take full advantage of their full potential, as it also

[17] Price and income can also be important determinant factors but which for the purpose of analysis can be defined, as customer needs. For example, the need to buy a low-priced product that is within one's income capabilities can be expressed as the need of the customer to seek a product that is "affordable" or simply "low cost".

condemned them to lack of access to the best raw materials and the latest technology and most importantly, deprived them of a truly competitive environment which would enable them to develop in a market driven way.

To describe a market performance gap, it is important to understand the dynamic nature of competition and the evolution of markets. Markets are driven by consumer needs. Although the basic human needs never change, the importance of each need depends on the situation of the consumer. For example, someone who is hungry is more likely to care about finding food than going to the opera. On the other hand, there is always a latent need for entertainment. The way people seek to satisfy this need can manifest itself in different forms and shapes. People develop expectations as to how they get satisfaction from a wide spectrum of product possibilities. These expectations are driven by technological advancements, information, life-style trends, and so on. The impact of these changes is that market expectations almost constantly shift across time and place. A business should fix its vision on clearly defined market needs and attempt to keep up with, as well as influence, the level and nature of market expectations.

Since market expectations are moving targets, it follows that the direction and size of market performance gaps also change constantly. It is the strong belief of the author that in the 1980s, there was a disorientation of business thinking away from this simple fact of life. What is of vital importance is the endeavour of a firm to pursue the fulfilment of customer expectations and where possible to help shape them in a way that affords it a sustainable competitive advantage. The pre-occupation of looking at "industries" and checking oneself with its "perceived close competitors" should never take precedence over an enterprise's attempt to understand, shape and satisfy the market expectations of its customers[18].

A successful new product should capture the imagination of the consumer. But to do that, it is necessary that one understands both the needs of the potential customer and the way that technology and other economic resources can be employed to bring about the desired result. A competitor can attempt to fill a market performance gap by employing to his advantage several critical supply-side success factors. The nature of the project and its environment affects, in broad terms, the allocation of weights of importance for such factors. For example, "scale" and "distribution leverages" are vital factors for success in the beer industry when one considers the economic

[18] Those market segments that happen to bear the market need that it is the business mission of the company to serve.

logistics of fast-moving consumer products. This does not mean, however, that a project without scale or distribution advantages cannot compete successfully in the beer market. Small breweries, for example, managing to "differentiate" their brands can also be successful because of adopting a competitive strategy more suited to their capabilities and the special needs of specific market segments.

A project can aim to use available resources to create capabilities[19] such as "scale", "distribution coverage", "information", "flexibility and responsiveness" and so on, to create product features which are likely to give it a competitive edge in the market. Sources of project capabilities may be found in many areas. The list is endless:

- *Technology factors*: Advanced production technology, flexibility of supply, efficient processing of information, purchasing economics, production economies, patents, licences.
- *Human factors*: Labour skills, experience, motivation, knowledge areas, training quality, creativity and culture, an efficient organisational structure, management quality and expertise, quick decision-making, corporate synergies,
- *Other factors*: Access to capital, efficient internal communication channels, market leadership in related markets, joint-ventures, successful related products, strong institutional image and advertising effectiveness, an efficient/wide distribution channel coverage, good relations with agents, exclusive agencies, superior service ability.

What is important is to identify in the analysis those resource areas that the project can attain access to and use them to form design solutions that meet market-need requirements. One should formulate a "winning marketing proposition" to tap the opportunities presented by an identified market performance gap. Levitt (1960) cites the example of Henry Ford who is today "wrongly" remembered more as a production rather than a marketing genius. Henry Ford's brilliance was in identifying a huge market performance gap and conceiving a winning marketing proposition that was feasible to take advantage of it. As Levitt points out in his classic paper "Marketing Myopia" Henry Ford "... actually invented the assembly line because he had concluded that at $500, he could sell millions of cars. Mass production was the *result* not the cause of his low prices."

[19] A capability is simply the use of a resource, or combination of resources, in a format that can satisfy market needs.

The project competitiveness

The competitiveness of a project is assessed through a process of disaggregating demand and supply with respect to the market need that the project aims to satisfy and setting market segments and competitor sets against the main consumer choice factors, as illustrated in the diagram (Figure 32).

Figure 32 - Marketing as a business system

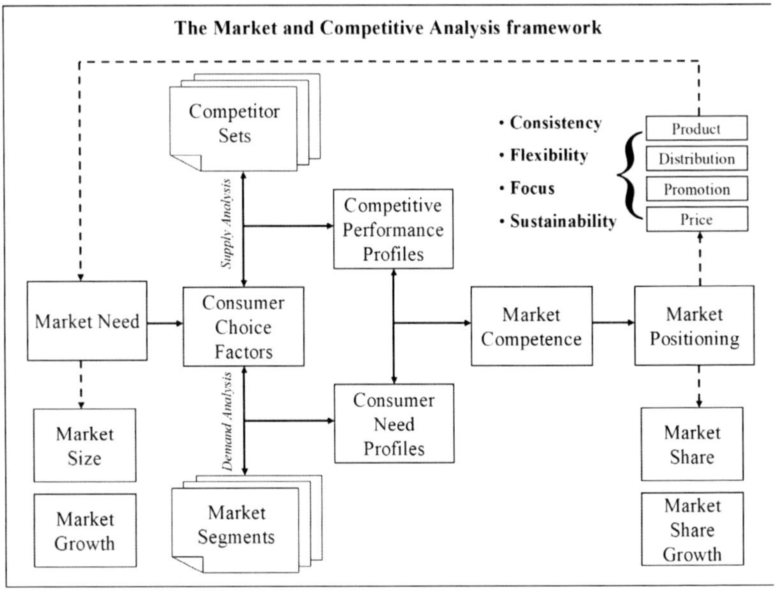

Consumer choice factors are the basic criteria on which the decision of which product or service to buy is taken by consumers participating, or likely to be participating, in the project's market. Consumer need profiles are extracted by adjusting for the relative importance attached to these factors by the identified market segments. The capacity of the competing products to satisfy the consumer choice factors enables the creation of competitive performance profiles. Market competence is simply the ability of the project to perform as well or better than other competitors on any of the key consumer choice factors. A competitive edge is therefore considered to be the capability to outscore other competitors with respect to a market segment. Market positioning is the direction of the project supply, or more precisely the marketing mix of the project, towards those market segments which maximise in terms of return the organisation's investment and inherent capabilities.

Market size and market growth are estimated in the context of the demand and supply analysis based on the project relevant market. Market share is taken to be the relative project supply adjusted by an estimate of the project competitive edge (positive or negative) in each targeted market segment. Finally, considerations regarding the project's organisation ability to adapt itself to market expectations and changing market conditions should drive the projected estimates for market share growth.

The perpetual race for competitiveness

The market is a competitive arena. It may be thought of as an athletic track where the "finish line" moves away from you the more you try to reach it. The positions of the runners (the competitors) in the race are determined by the value of the benefits that their products and services offer to their customers. There are two special characteristics about the race for competitiveness. The first is that no matter how close one can get to the "finish line" one can never cross it and finish the race. This in effect means that one cannot exceed market expectations because the closer one gets, the more expectations one creates. People will always want more of what is possible for them to have. The second special characteristic is that the "finish line" is a moving target whose position can and <u>does</u> change because of a host of factors that influence people's preferences and the ability of suppliers to serve them such as technology, trends and fashion and government regulation or deregulation. But most importantly, market expectations change by the constantly evolving marketing mix offerings of competitors as well as that of the project itself.

The struggle to attain competitive position is therefore an on-going process whereby competitors try to narrow the gap between the value of the benefits contained in their products and services and the ever changing and increasing customer expectations. For this reason, the analysis is not merely an assessment of a static situation, for example, whether a product, as designed, is likely to outsell other market products, but rather, whether a project has those traits that will enable it to be, and remain, competitive come what may. A project appraisal should therefore cover questions such as whether a project can adopt a way of business by which to develop and institutionalise mechanisms that will enable it to monitor market needs, critically assess its own and other competitors' performance in serving them, develop the required market competencies, position (and reposition) its products in the market as necessary and keep itself on track for the duration of the life of the project[20].

The conceptual framework of the market competitive process in which a project operates is demonstrated in Figure 33:

Figure 33 - A market-based system for sustained competitiveness

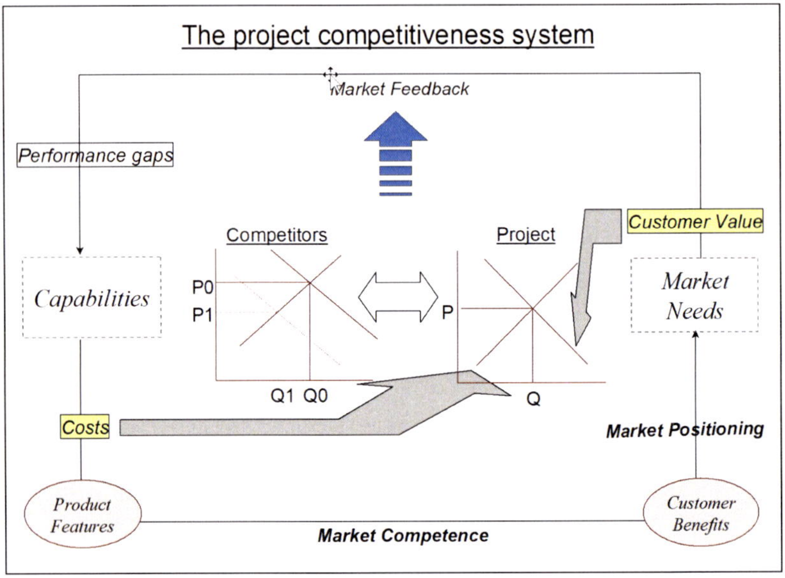

Project competitiveness is shown to be the continuous development and marketing of products and services through:

- The building up of a capability base through which to aim to generate customer benefits that satisfy the core market needs better than other competitors (market competence) and,
- The targeting and tuning of the marketing mix to the distinctive needs of specific market segments, which can derive the highest customer value from the product features that the enterprise is developing a market competence for (market positioning). This should take place within the context of the current market structure and possible reaction of other suppliers and potential new entrants.

[20] The management/owner of the project (e.g., the firm) should be capable of planning and developing new innovative products to replace the existing ones even after the projected life of the existing project.

While adding product features has a direct effect on the costs and supply function of the project, additional customer benefits cause an expansion of the project demand reflecting the increase in customer value. The impact of the project on existing competitors, as well as their possible reaction within the context of the current market structure, is an important factor in assessing the project's strategic position. Given a market feedback mechanism, the loop is completed with the identification of market performance gaps, which guide further investments and innovations, that aim towards outperforming the competition in satisfying market needs and creating loyal customers.

Market competence

Market competence is the learned or acquired ability of organisations to create and market product features, which can generate net customer benefits. In terms of the customer, a net customer benefit is when the additional customer value generated from a new set of product features is greater than the increase in price he will have to pay for it. In cash flow terms, this takes the form of a net financial gain that arises when the present value of the stream of benefits of a new project feature is greater than the present value of the costs incurred to produce and market it.

Market analysis should lead towards the building of alternative project formulations that attempt to combine the limited resources and capabilities attainable by the project in ways that can best address the basic market needs identified in the project relevant market. A competitive enterprise seeks to develop such skills and capabilities that will enable it to distinguish itself from other suppliers and yet remain flexible enough to respond quickly and effectively to changing market conditions as necessary. The selected areas of competence should therefore be such that it is possible to build upon and defend to ensure continued success in the market.

Market Positioning

Market positioning is the second set of wheels of the market performance wagon. It refers to the selection of a target market among the various market segments and the identification of a unique positioning for the project's products on the map of consumer perceptions of competing products in the market. McBurnie and Clutterbuck (1988) point out that:

> "[Positioning through] segmentation is fundamental to successful marketing strategies. Until competitors copy or segment your segmentation, you have

> a competitive edge, even if you serve the segment with a standard product or service. If the product is specific to the segment, then your competitive advantage is multiplied."

A project should select a target market based on its capabilities and the specific requirements and needs and behavioural characteristics of the market segments within the relevant market. Target marketing aims to optimise the ability of a business unit to satisfy market needs by concentrating its resources and efforts on serving, primarily, those market segments that attach the highest value to the customer benefits for which the project can attain market competence.

In selecting a target market, a project should maintain focus, consistency and flexibility. Focus refers to concentrating the efforts of the business on providing a good product and service that caters well for the needs of the core market segment rather than spreading itself thin to serve all possible customers. Consistency basically means not trying to serve a second or third market segment where this will constrain the ability of the project to serve the core market segments well. Flexibility is about selecting a strategic positioning which will make it relatively easy and less costly to change if things do not turn out the way it is expected.

Essentially, targeting is a question of setting priorities among the various market segments within the relevant market. A targeted market can therefore consist of many market segments. In including a market segment in the target market of a project, one should however ensure that its presence does not obstruct the effective delivery of a superior product in segments with higher priority. It is not very effective, for example, for a cruise ship to target and hope to serve equally as well vacationers and commuters seeking a cheap mode of travel. One should focus marketing efforts on those consumer groups whose needs are a better match to the customer benefits that can be generated by the project's products.

To optimise the positioning of a product in the market, it is necessary to understand how consumers map the existing products in their mind. In other words, what are the criteria, or factors, against which consumers choose a brand in the market and how do the main competing brands rate against these key dimensions of choice. Many companies spend big sums of money in researching consumer perceptions to derive perceptual maps.

Figure 34 - Perceptual mapping

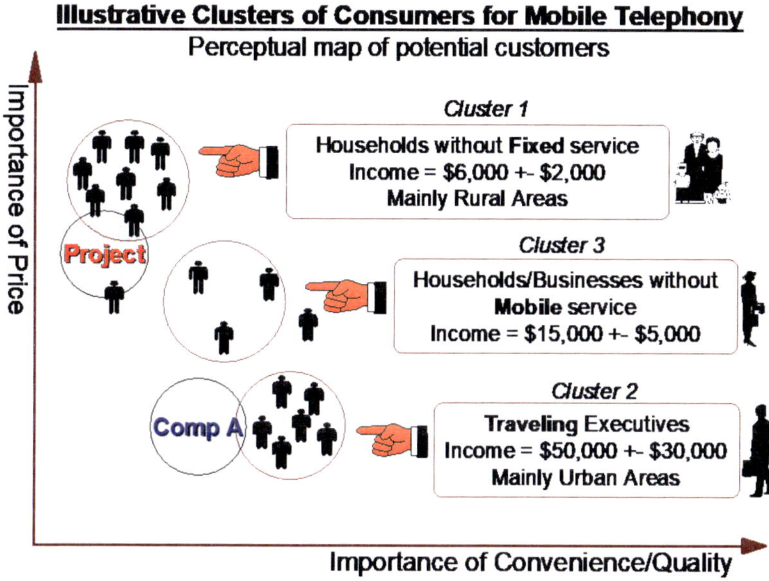

A perceptual map can be a useful tool for interpreting how consumers differentiate competing products and how the project may position its products to gain a competitive advantage. The analyst uses the main two (or on rare occasions three) market need factors to form crossing axes. These represent the dimensions of choice as perceived by consumers. Positioning a competing product on the chart is simple in a two-dimensional grid, difficult on a three-dimensional grid and impossible to plot on a single chart if more than three factors are used. When perceptual positioning is combined with customer profile information then its strategic significance increases substantially, as it is demonstrated in the example below, which maps two competing satellite cellular telephone products.

Analysing the characteristics of the three main clusters it was found that each product was appealing to distinctly different customer profiles. The characteristics of the project's product were a very close match to the perceptual position of consumers in Cluster 1. The company promoting the project would therefore be more effective in targeting this market segment rather than following a generic strategy of addressing all market segments.

The process of collecting and processing information to create perceptual maps can be very sophisticated and costly. Large companies, involved mostly in consumer products, spend a substantial part of their marketing budget for this purpose. Although it is generally recognised that there can be no survey technique, statistical method or computer program that measures consumer perceptions accurately, perceptual mapping is still used extensively because it serves as a useful conceptual tool aiding the formulation of strategy. Moreover, it can communicate and make explicit the analyst's understanding of the market situation.

Measuring project competitiveness

Identifying key product features provides the basis for projecting costs and revenues. In order to assess the likely impact of a planned bundle of product features on the projected revenues, one should attempt to answer the question "how well can these features satisfy the identified market needs"? Will they generate such customer benefits that will be perceived as more gratifying than the benefits generated by the products and services of competing suppliers? What would be the additional costs, in capital and operating expenditure, necessary to introduce such features?

The competitive strategy of a project finds an expression in the market through the marketing mix. The marketing mix refers to the market offering of a firm reflecting its total efforts in making its product as competitive as possible. It involves the *product* aspects, its *promotion* or communication mix, *distribution* coverage and, of course, *pricing*. The latter is determined by the simple demand and supply model after considering the impact of the other marketing mix elements on the project supply and demand.

To assess the project demand and supply conditions it is necessary to consider the effect of the marketing assumptions regarding the selected competitive strategy on *supplier costs* and the *customer value* generation ability of the project's marketing mix. Apart from *price*, which is the subject of analysis of micro-economic theory, the other three elements of a marketing mix (product, promotion and distribution) correspond and change the underlying assumptions of the simple demand and supply model of *product homogeneity*, *perfect information* and *perfect access* to the market.

Figure 35 - Marketing and Economic Theory

The Project Marketing Mix and Economic Theory

Marketing mix element		Economic theory assumption
•Product mix	⟺	•Homogeneity
•Promotion mix	⟺	•Perfect Information
•Distribution mix	⟺	•Perfect Access
•Price mix	⟺	•Market structure

The marketing mix components are the levers that a company uses to make its product more competitive in the market. The product mix has to do with the positioning and design of the product to make it most appealing to a targeted market. The primary management issue is to identify the perceptual dimensions of choice of consumers and the selection of a strategic position of the company's products considering its own capabilities, as well as the position and capabilities of its competitors (see market positioning above). The promotion mix relates to the costs and effectiveness of advertising and sales promotion campaigns, through which a company chooses to make its targeted customers aware of their products, stimulate their interest and reinforce/strengthen the positive attitudes of existing customers. The primary management decision for an effective promotion policy is the adoption of the right advertising message (and sales promotion schemes) and the cost-effective selection of the advertising and promotion media. The distribution mix involves the decision regarding which channels and how much coverage is necessary to efficiently carry the product to the customer (make it easily accessible to its targeted market).

The main determinants of effectiveness for each of the marketing mix elements are illustrated in Figure 36.

Price and quantity are the result of *supplier costs* and generated *customer value* (effective demand) as well as *market structure*, which are related to the assumptions regarding the *product*, *promotion* and *distribution* mixes.

The usefulness of considering the determinants of effectiveness of the marketing mix elements in a cash flow projection context is that it imposes a discipline by which aspects of project competitiveness are considered in an explicit manner thereby containing the build-up of inconsistent marketing scenarios for the project.

Figure 36 - Optimising the marketing mix

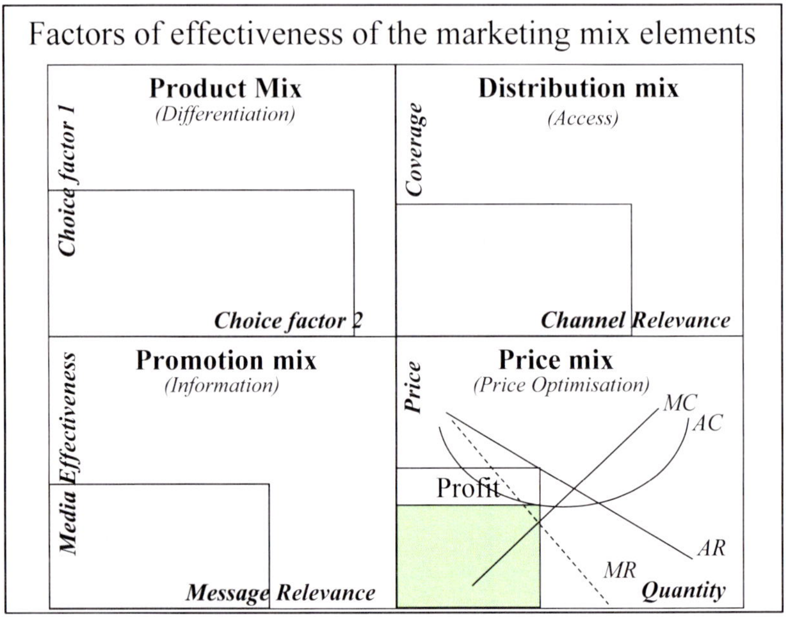

Organisational aspects of competitiveness

Project competitiveness is a function of both the characteristics of the *product* and the *system* that develops it. The management and business orientation of the firm undertaking the project partly determines the dynamic system in which the project will exist and as such it invariably becomes a critical factor of competitiveness for the project itself. The characteristics of companies that consistently show the highest returns (based on the data provided by hundreds of companies to the "Profit impact of Market Strategy" - PIMS research)[21] as noted by McBurnie and Clutterbuck (1988) are:

> "... picking viable [market] niches, achieving a leadership position within them and providing a high value-added product or service".

[21] The Strategic Planning Institute of Cambridge, Massachusetts.

To consider the ability of a project to attain and sustain a leadership position, it is necessary to view the project as a subset of a bigger system; the organisation.

As a system, a competitive project should form part of an organisation, which has:

- A clearly defined business mission. One that correctly reflects the underlying market need served and the key area of competence of the organisation.
- A learning mechanism and flexible organisational structure by which to monitor and quickly respond to opportunities in its market environment.
- A management leadership that believes in serving the customer and is committed to instilling a customer philosophy at all the levels of the organisation.
- An integrated organisation where all employees, no matter how diverse in their skills and tasks, work towards a common goal while realising and respecting their inter-dependence in achieving the corporate objective.

The above is by no means an exhaustive list of the characteristics of a competitive organisation. It is not possible to do justice to the topic in this space. One should bear in mind, however, that unless evidence of such traits of organisational competitiveness exists, the very foundation of the appraisal might be questionable.

The analysis should lead towards a clear definition of the project's competitive advantage. A competitive advantage statement should consider the possible changes in the project's environment and how exposed to competition are its market competencies. It should be tested against the ability of the management of the project to sustain a competitive edge under changing market conditions and the existence of key factors that are likely to make the project a lasting success. The statement should mention which are the market competencies that can be created by the project and how the products of the project are to be positioned in the market so that high customer value is achieved. The project return is the natural consequence of these factors, and it should simply be a quantification of the above assumptions that is reflected in the bottom line of the cash-flow projections.

Conclusion

"Marketing analysis and competitiveness in project appraisal" describes a need, and, hopefully, raises a few questions more than it provides answers for the project analyst. It sketches the elements and concerns that should be paramount in the mind of a diligent researcher who, through his cash flow projections, aims to gain a better understanding of the project and its environment. It encourages an inter-active approach towards investment appraisal, which can often lead towards better project design. The investment appraisal model enhanced by a thoughtful marketing evaluation is not merely the end product of analysis but also becomes a vehicle for arriving at better investment plans.

To check the validity of the assumptions in a cash flow projection one should be able to provide answers to the following questions:

What is the market need that the project aims to satisfy?

What is the project's relevant market?

What is the market size?

How is the market segmented? (How are the market-need profiles of the various segments different?).

Who are the project's prime competitors? (What are they good or bad at?).

Which are the project capabilities? (What market competencies can the project develop?).

What is the project's target market? (Is it consistent and focused enough?).

What is the market performance gap that the project will fill? (How is the project positioned in the market?).

What is the project's competitive advantage? (Is it sustainable?).

Will the project generate a market expansion? (Is this reflected in the cash flow projections?).

Are the cash flow projections consistent with the marketing analysis and strategic positioning of the project?

It has been the experience of the author that most project analysts cannot provide any type of answer to half of the above questions. Yet, in retrospect it is often conceded that it is at least as important to have good answers to these questions as it is mastering and applying the correct methodologies in project appraisal.

The formulation of the project appraisal marketing-module problem in the context of a conceptual framework of marketing analysis facilitates project design, the identification of market competencies and the strategic positioning of the project in its market. Irrespective of how accurate the market profiles are, or indeed can be, the marketing analysis framework imposes a discipline that makes the analyst search for solutions that are strategically and marketing-wise consistent with his assumptions and understanding of the market. The process itself often leads, or should lead, one towards a re-formulation and a more optimal design of the project that is being appraised.

IV. Risk Analysis in Investment Appraisal

*Based on an article published by Savvides, S., "**Project Appraisal**", Volume 9 Number 1, pages 3-18, March 1994, © Beech Tree Publishing 1994 and* ***Republished*** *in the book:* ***Cost–Benefit Analysis for Investment Decisions*** *(The International Library of Critical Writings in Economics series, 152) by Harberger A., Jenkins G., Kuo C., by Edward Elgar Publishing (December 29, 2018)*

Project uncertainty

The purpose of investment appraisal is to assess the economic prospects of a proposed investment project. It is a methodology for calculating the expected return based on cash-flow forecasts of many, often inter-related, project variables. Risk emanates from the uncertainty encompassing these projected variables. The evaluation of project risk therefore depends on the one hand, on our ability to identify and understand the nature of uncertainty surrounding the key project variables and on the other, on having the tools and methodology to process its risk implications on the return of the project.

The first task of project evaluation is to estimate the future values of the projected variables. Generally, we utilise information regarding a specific event of the past to predict a possible future outcome of the same or similar event. The approach usually employed in investment appraisal is to calculate a "best estimate" based on the available data and use it as an input in the evaluation model. These single-value estimates are usually the mode[22] (the most likely outcome), the average or a conservative estimate[23].

In selecting a single value however, a range of other probable outcomes for each project variable (data which are often of vital importance to the investment decision as they pertain to the risk aspects of the project) are not

[22] Even if one uses the most likely value of every project variable it does not mean that the derived result will also be the most likely result (See Reutlinger, 1970, pages 25-26).

[23] A value below the most likely estimate for a variable whose impact on the cash flow of the project is positive (such as quantity sold) or a value above the most likely estimate for a variable whose impact on the net cash flow of the project is negative (such as payroll cost).

included in the analysis. By relying completely on single values as inputs it is implicitly assumed that the values used in the appraisal are certain. The outcome of the project is, therefore, also presented as a certainty with no possible variance or margin of error associated with it.

Recognising the fact that the values projected are not certain, an appraisal report is usually supplemented to include sensitivity and scenario analysis tests. Sensitivity analysis, in its simplest form, involves changing the value of a variable to test its impact on the final result. It is therefore used to identify the project's most important, highly sensitive, variables.

Scenario analysis remedies one of the shortcomings of sensitivity analysis[24] by allowing the simultaneous change of values for a number of key project variables thereby constructing an alternative scenario for the project. Pessimistic and optimistic scenarios are usually presented.

Sensitivity and scenario analyses compensate mostly for the analytical limitation of having to straightjacket a host of possibilities into single numbers. However, both tests are static and rather arbitrary in their nature.

The use of risk analysis in investment appraisal carries sensitivity and scenario analyses through to their logical conclusion. Monte Carlo simulation adds the dimension of dynamic analysis to project evaluation by making it possible build up random scenarios which are consistent with the analyst's key assumptions about risk. A risk analysis application utilises a wealth of information, be it in the form of objective data or expert opinion, to quantitatively describe the uncertainty surrounding the key project variables as probability distributions, and to calculate in a consistent manner its possible impact on the expected return of the project.

The output of a risk analysis is not single-values but probability distributions of all possible expected returns. The prospective investor is therefore provided with a complete risk/return profile of the project showing all the possible outcomes that could result from the decision to stake his money on a particular investment project.

Risk analysis computer programs are mere tools for overcoming the processing limitations which have been containing investment decisions to be made solely on single-value (or "certainty equivalent") projections. One of the reasons why risk analysis was not, until recently, frequently applied

[24] Changing the value of only one project variable may create an unrealistic scenario because the variable may be correlated with other input variables.

is that micro-computers were not powerful enough to handle the demanding needs of Monte Carlo simulation and because a tailor-made project appraisal computer model had to be developed for each case as part and parcel of the risk analysis application.

This was rather expensive and time consuming, especially considering that it had to be developed on main-frame or mini computers, often using low level computer languages. However, with the rapid leaps achieved in micro-computer technology, both in hardware and software, it is now possible to develop risk analysis programs that can be applied generically, and with ease, to any investment appraisal model.

Risk analysis is not a substitute for normal investment appraisal methodology but rather a tool that enhances its results. A good appraisal model is a necessary base on which to set up a meaningful simulation. Risk analysis supports the investment decision by giving the investor a measure of the variance associated with a project appraisal return estimate.

By being essentially a decision-making tool, risk analysis has many applications and functions that extend its usefulness beyond pure investment appraisal decisions. It can also develop into a powerful decision-making device in marketing, strategic management, economics, financial budgeting, production management and in many other fields in which relationships that are based on uncertain variables are modelled to facilitate and enhance the decision-making process.

The Risk Analysis Process

What is risk analysis?

Risk analysis, or "probabilistic simulation" based on the Monte Carlo simulation technique is methodology by which the uncertainty encompassing the main variables projected in a forecasting model is processed to estimate the impact of risk on the projected results. It is a technique by which a mathematical model is subjected to a number of simulations, usually with the aid of a computer. During the simulation process, successive scenarios are built up using input values for the project's key uncertain variables which are selected from multi-value probability distributions.

The simulation is controlled so that the random selection of values from the specified probability distributions does not violate the existence of known or suspected correlation relationships among the project variables. The results are collected and analysed statistically to arrive at a probability distribution of the potential outcomes of the project and to estimate various measures of project risk.

The risk analysis process can be broken down into the following stages as shown in Figure 37.

Figure 37 - The Risk Analysis Process

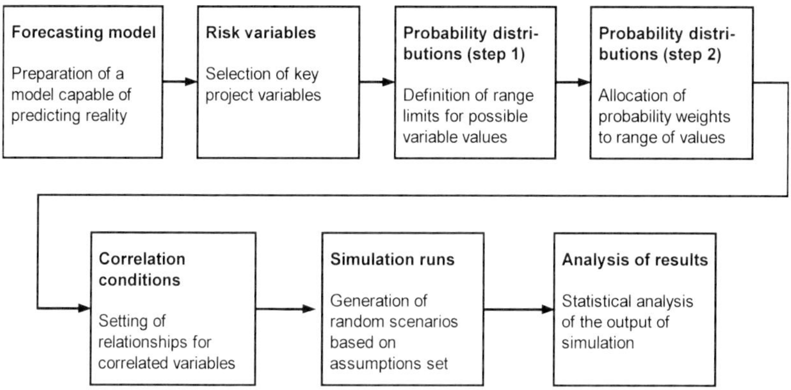

Forecasting model

The first stage of a risk analysis application is simply the requirement for a robust model capable of predicting correctly if fed with the correct data. This involves the creation of a forecasting model (often using a computer), which defines the mathematical relationships between numerical variables that relate to forecasts of the future. It is a set of formulae that process several input variables to arrive at a result. One of the simplest models possible is a single relationship between two variables. For example, if B=Benefits and C=Costs, then perhaps the simplest investment appraisal model is as in Figure 38:

Figure 38 - A simple model

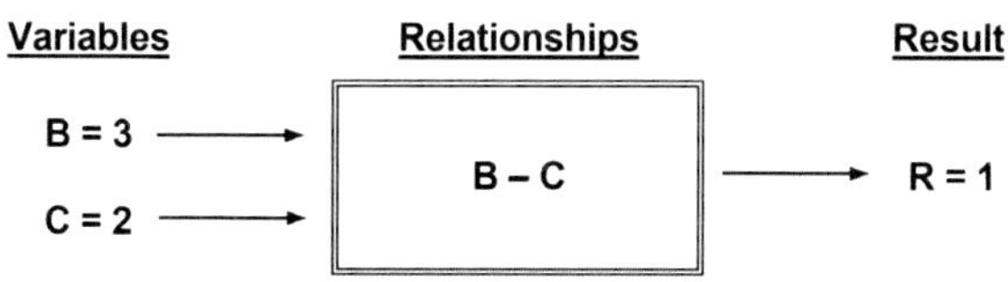

A good model is one that includes all the relevant variables (and excludes all non-relevant ones) and postulates the correct relationships between them.

Consider the forecasting model in Figure 39 which is a very simple cash flow statement containing projections of only one year[25]. It shows how the result of the model (the net cash flow) formula depends on the values of other variables, the values generated by formulae and the relationship between them. The model is made up of five variables and five formulae. Notice that there are formulae that process the result of other formulae as well as simple input variables (for instance formula F4). We will be using this simple appraisal model to illustrate the risk analysis process.

Figure 39 - Forecasting model

Forecasting Model

	$	Variables	Formulae
Sales price	12	V1	
Volume of sales	100	V2	
Cash inflow	1,200		F1 = V1 × V2
Materials	300		F2 = V2 × V4
Wages	400		F3 = V2 × V5
Expenses	200	V3	
Cash outflow	900		F4 = F2 + F3 + V3
Net Cash Flow	300		F5 = F1 – F4
Relevant assumptions			
Material cost per unit	3.00	V4	
Wages per unit	4.00	V5	

[25] A one-year cash-flow, rather than a fully projected cash-flow statement, is used to demonstrate as simply as possible the stages of a risk analysis application. It is assumed that the project is a once-off venture where there is no upfront capital investment or residual values (for instance producing and selling apple pies to sell in a major one-time event such as the Olympic Games).

Risk variables

The second stage entails the selection of the model's "risk variables". A risk variable is defined as one which is critical to the viability of the project in the sense that a small deviation from its projected value is both probable and potentially damaging to the project worth. To select risk variables, we apply sensitivity and uncertainty analysis.

Sensitivity analysis is used in risk analysis to identify the most important variables in a project appraisal model. It measures the responsiveness of the project result vis-à-vis a change (usually a fixed percentage deviation) in the value of a given project variable.

The problem with sensitivity analysis as it is applied in practice is that there are no rules as to the extent to which a change in the value of a variable is tested for its impact on the projected result. For example, a 10% increase in labour costs may be very likely to occur while a 10% increase in sales revenue may be very unlikely. The sensitivity test applied uniformly on several project variables does not take into account how realistic or unrealistic the projected change in the value of a tested variable is.

For sensitivity analysis to yield meaningful results, the impact of uncertainty should be incorporated into the test. Uncertainty analysis is the attainment of some understanding of the type and magnitude of uncertainty encompassing the variables to be tested and using it to select risk variables. For instance, it may be found that a small deviation in the purchase price of a given piece of machinery at year 0 is very significant to the project return. The likelihood, however, of even such a small deviation taking place may be extremely slim if the supplier is contractually obliged and bound by guarantees to supply at the agreed price. The risk associated with this variable is therefore insignificant even though the project result is very sensitive to it. Conversely, a project variable with high uncertainty should not be included in the probabilistic analysis unless its impact on the project result, within the expected margins of uncertainty, is significant.

The reason for including only the most crucial variables in a risk analysis application is twofold. First, the greater the number of probability distributions employed in a random simulation, the higher the likelihood of generating inconsistent scenarios because of the difficulty in setting and monitoring relationships for correlated variables (see Correlated variables below).

Second, the cost (in terms of expert time and money) needed to define accurate probability distributions and correlation conditions for many variables with a small possible impact on the result is likely to outweigh any benefit to be derived. Hence, rather than extending the breadth of analysis to cover a larger number of project variables, it is more productive to focus attention and available resources on adding more depth to the assumptions regarding the few most sensitive and uncertain variables in a project.

In our simple appraisal model (Figure 40) we have identified three risk variables. The price and volume of sales, because these are expected to be determined by the demand and supply conditions at the time the project will operate, and the cost of materials per unit, because the price of apples, the main material to be used, could vary substantially, again, depending on market conditions at the time of purchase. All three variables when tested within their respected margins of uncertainty, were found to affect the outcome of the project significantly.

Figure 40 - Sensitivity and uncertainty analysis

Sensitivity and uncertainty analysis

	$	Risk variables	
Sales price	12	V1	⬅
Volume of sales	100	V2	⬅
Cash inflow	1,200		
Materials	300		
Wages	400		
Expenses	200		
Cash outflow	900		
Net Cash Flow	300		
Relevant assumptions			
Material cost per unit	3.00	V4	⬅
Wages per unit	4.00		

Probability distributions

Defining uncertainty

Although the future is by definition "uncertain" we can still anticipate the outcome of future events. We can very accurately predict, for example, the exact time at which daylight breaks at some part of the world for a particular day of the year. We can do this because we have gathered millions of observations of the event which confirm the accuracy of the prediction. On the other hand, it is very difficult for us to forecast with great accuracy the rate of general inflation next year or the occupancy rate to be attained by a new hotel project in the first year of its operation.

There are many factors that govern our ability to forecast accurately a future event. These relate to the complexity of the system determining the outcome of a variable and the sources of uncertainty it depends on. Our ability to narrow the margins of uncertainty of a forecast therefore depends on our understanding of the nature and level of uncertainty regarding the variable in question and the quality and quantity of information available at the time of the assessment. Often such information is embedded in the experience of the person making the prediction. It is only very rarely possible, or indeed cost effective, to conduct statistical analysis on a set of objective data for the purpose of estimating the future value of a variable used in the appraisal of a project[26].

In defining the uncertainty encompassing a given project variable one should widen the uncertainty margins to account for the lack of sufficient data or the inherent errors contained in the base data used in making the prediction. While it is almost impossible to forecast accurately the actual value that a variable may assume sometime in the future, it should be quite possible to include the true value within the limits of a sufficiently wide probability distribution. The analyst should make use of the available data and expert opinion to define a range of values and probabilities that can capture the outcome of the future event in question.

The preparation of a probability distribution for the selected project variable involves setting up a range of values and allocating probability weights to it. Although we refer to these two stages in turn, it must be emphasised that in practice the definition of a probability distribution is an iterative process. Range values are specified having in mind a particular probability profile, while the definition of a range of values for a risk variable often influences

[26] Where this is possible the accuracy of the prediction will be higher under the following conditions:

- the greater the similarity of the data used to the variable to be forecast
- the bigger the sample of data
- the lower the variation of values in the data used
- the shorter the period of extrapolation from the base data.

the decision regarding the allocation of probability.

Setting range limits

The level of variation possible for each identified risk variable is specified through the setting of limits (minimum and maximum values). Thus, a range of possible values for each risk variable is defined which sets boundaries around the value that a projected variable may assume.

The definition of value range limits for project variables may seem to be a difficult task to someone applying risk analysis for the first time. It should, however, be no more difficult than the assignment of a single-value best estimate. In deterministic appraisal, the probable values that a project variable may take still have to be considered, before selecting one to use as an input in the appraisal.

Therefore, if a thoughtful assessment of the single-value estimate has taken place, most of the preparatory work for setting range limits for a probability distribution for that variable must have already been done. In practice, the problem faced in attempting to define probability distributions for risk analysis subsequently to the completion of a base case scenario is the realisation that not sufficient thought and research has gone into the single-value estimate in the first place.

When data are available, the definition of range limits for project variables is a simple process of processing the data to arrive at a probability distribution. For example, looking at historical observations of an event it is possible to organise the information in the form of a frequency distribution. This may be derived by grouping the number of occurrences of each outcome at consecutive value intervals. The probability distribution in such a case is the frequency distribution itself with frequencies expressed in relative rather than absolute terms (values ranging from 0 to 1 where the total sum must be equal to 1). This process is illustrated in Figure 41.

It is seldom possible to have, or to afford the cost of purchasing, quantitative information which will enable the definition of range values and the allocation of probability weights for a risk variable on totally objective criteria. It is usually necessary to rely on judgement and subjective factors for determining the most likely values of a project appraisal variable. In such a situation the method suggested is to survey the opinion of experts (or in the absence of experts of people who can have some intelligible feel of the subject).

Figure 41 - From a frequency to a probability distribution

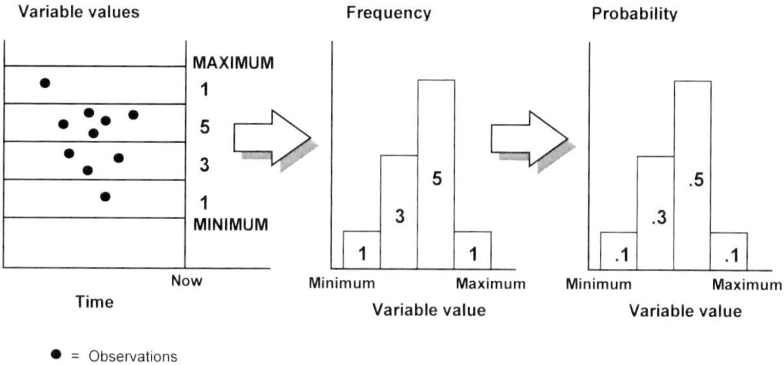

The analyst should attempt to gather responses to the question "what values are considered to be the highest and lowest possible for a given risk variable". If the probability distribution to be attached to the set range of values (see allocating probability below) is one which concentrates probability towards the middle values of the range (for example the normal probability distribution), it may be better to opt for the widest range limits mentioned. If, on the other hand, the probability distribution to be used is one that allocates probability evenly across the range limits considered (for instance the uniform probability distribution) then the most likely or even one of the narrower range limits considered may be more appropriate.

In the final analysis the definition of range limits rests on the good judgement of the analyst. He should be able to understand and justify the choices made. It should be apparent, however, that the decision on the definition of a range of values is not independent of the decision regarding the allocation of probability.

Allocating probability

Each value within the defined range limits has an equal chance of occurrence. Probability distributions are used to regulate the likelihood of selection of values within the defined ranges.

The need to employ probability distributions stems from the fact that an attempt is being made to forecast a future event, not because risk analysis is being applied. Conventional investment appraisal uses one particular type of probability distribution for all the project variables included in the appraisal model. It is called the deterministic probability distribution and is one that assigns all probability to a single value.

Figure 42 - Forecasting the outcome of a future event: single-value estimate

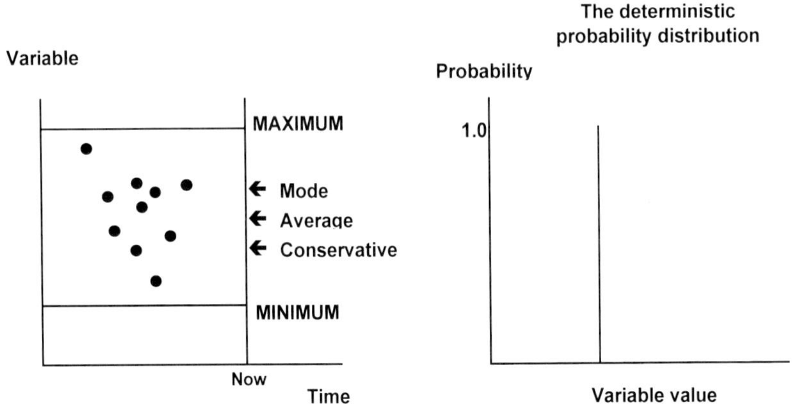

In assessing the data available for a project variable, as illustrated in the example in Figure 42, the analyst is constrained to selecting only one out of the many outcomes possible, or to calculate a summary measure (be it the mode, the average, or just a conservative estimate). The assumption then must be made that the selected value is certain to occur (assigning a probability of 1 to the chosen single-value best estimate). Since this probability distribution has only one outcome, the result of the appraisal model can be determined in one calculation (or one simulation run). Hence, conventional project evaluation is sometimes referred to as deterministic analysis.

In the application of risk analysis, the richer and wider information contained within multi-value probability distributions is utilised. The fact that risk analysis uses multi-value instead of deterministic probability distributions for the risk variables to feed the appraisal model with the data is what distinguishes the simulation from the deterministic (or conventional) approach to project evaluation. Some of the probability distributions used in the application of risk analysis are illustrated in Figure 43.

Figure 43 - Multi-value probability distributions

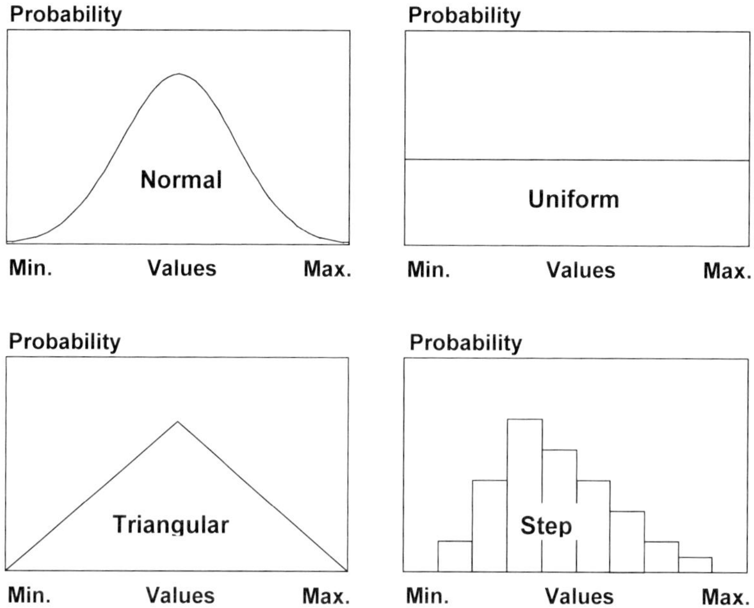

The allocation of probability weights to values within the minimum and maximum range limits involves the selection of a suitable probability distribution profile or the specific attachment of probability weights to values (or intervals within the range).

Probability distributions are used to express quantitatively the beliefs and expectations of experts regarding the outcome of a particular future event. People who have this expertise are usually able to judge which one of these devices best expresses their knowledge about the subject. We can distinguish between two basic categories of probability distributions.

First, there are various types of symmetrical distributions. For example, the normal, uniform, and triangular probability distributions allocate probability symmetrically across the defined range but with varying degrees of concentration towards the middle values. The variability profile of many project variables can usually be adequately described using one such symmetrical distribution. Symmetrical distributions are more appropriate in situations for which the final outcome of the projected variable is likely to be determined by the interplay of equally important counteracting forces on both sides of the range limits defined; like for example the price of a product as determined in a competitive market environment (such as the sales price of apple pies in our simple example).

The second category of probability distributions are the step and skewed distributions. With a step distribution one can define range intervals giving each its own probability weight in a step-like manner (as illustrated in Figure 43). The step distribution is particularly useful if expert opinion is abundant. It is more suitable in situations where one-sided rigidities exist in the system that determines the outcome of the projected variable. Such a situation may arise where an extreme value within the defined range is the most likely outcome[27].

Correlated variables

Identifying and attaching appropriate probability distributions to risk variables is fundamental in a risk analysis application. Having completed these two steps and with the aid of a reliable computer programme[28] it is technically possible to advance to the simulation stage in which the computer builds up several project scenarios based on random input values generated from the specified probability distributions (see Simulation runs below). However, proceeding straight to a simulation would be correct only if no significant correlations exist among any of the selected risk variables.

The correlation problem

Two or more variables are said to be correlated if they tend to vary together in a systematic manner. It is not uncommon to have such relationships in a set of risk variables. For example, the level of operating costs would, to a large extent, drive sales price or the price of a product would usually be expected to have an inverse effect on the volume of sales. The precise nature of such relationships is often unknown and cannot be specified with a great deal of accuracy as it is simply a conjecture of what may happen in the

---

[27] For example, the projected inflation rate of a country for a particular year may be only 2% with very low probability of dropping further; yet it is considered quite probable for the inflation rate to increase up to 7%, if popular economic measures which can cause inflationary pressures on the economy materialise.

[28] 'RiskMaster', later renamed 'RiskEase", by Master Solutions is one such software package. It is an add-in software that works with Microsoft Excel to provide risk analysis capability. The software application was originally developed by the author for the Harvard University Program in Investment Appraisal and Management (PIAM) and applies the concepts presented in this paper.

future.

The existence of correlated variables among the designated risk variables can, however, distort the results of risk analysis. The reason for this is that the selection of input values from the assigned probability distributions for each variable is purely random. It is therefore possible that the resultant inputs generated for some scenarios violate a systematic relationship that may exist between two or more variables. To give an example, suppose that market price and quantity are both included as risk variables in a risk analysis application. It is reasonable to expect some negative covariance between the two variables (that is, when the price is high quantity is more likely to assume a low value and vice versa). Without restricting the random generation of values from the corresponding probability distributions defined for the two variables, it is almost sure that some of the scenarios generated would not conform to this expectation of the analyst which would result in unrealistic scenarios where price and quantity are both high, or both low.

The existence of inconsistent scenarios in a sample of simulation runs means that the results of risk analysis will be to some extent biased or off target. Before proceeding to the simulation runs stage, it is therefore imperative to consider whether such relationships exist among the defined risk variables and, where necessary, to provide such constraints to the model that the possibility of generating scenarios that violate these correlations is diminished. In effect, setting correlation conditions restricts the random selection of values for correlated variables so that it is confined within the direction and limits of their expected dependency characteristics.

Practical solution

One way of dealing with the correlation problem in a risk analysis application is to use the correlation coefficient as an indication, or proxy, of the relationship between two risk variables. The analyst therefore indicates the direction of the projected relationship and an estimate (often a reasonable guess) of the strength of association between the two projected correlated variables. The purpose of the exercise is to contain the model from generating grossly inconsistent scenarios rather than attaining high statistical accuracy. It is therefore sufficient to assume that the relationship is linear and that it is expressed in the formula:

$$Y = a + bX + e$$

where:

Y	= dependent variable,
X	= independent variable
a (intercept)	= the minimum Y value (if relationship is positive) or,
	= the maximum Y value (if relationship is negative),
b (slope)	$= \frac{(\text{maximum } Y \text{ value } - \text{ minimum } Y \text{ value})}{(\text{maximum } X \text{ value } - \text{ minimum } X \text{ value})}$,
e (error factor)	= independently distributed normal errors.

It is important to realise that the use of the correlation coefficient suggested here is simply that of a device by which the analyst can express a suspected relationship between two risk variables. The task of the computer programme is to try to adhere, as much as possible, to that condition[29]. The object of the correlation analysis is to control the values of the dependent variable so that a consistency is maintained with their counter values of the independent variable.

The regression equation forms part of the assumptions that regulate this relationship during a simulation process. As shown in the formula explanation above, the intercept and the slope, the two parameters of a linear regression, are implicitly defined at the time the minimum and maximum possible values for the two correlated variables are specified. Given these assumptions the analyst only must define the polarity of the relationship (whether it is positive or negative) and the correlation coefficient (r) which is a value from 0 to 1[30].

In our simple example one negative relationship is imposed on the model. This aims at containing the possibility of quantity sold responding positively (in the same direction) to a change in price. Price (V1) is the independent variable and Volume of sales (V2) is the dependent variable. The two variables are assumed to be negatively correlated by a coefficient (r) of -0.8. The completed simulation model including the setting for correlations is

[29] Correlation analysis is usually employed to analyse a set of data to facilitate the prediction of the dependent variable from actual (or hypothetical) values of the independent variable where the regression equation and the correlation coefficient are the outputs of such analysis. In the risk analysis application described here these are merely the inputs, while the output is the generated data for the dependent variable during the simulation process.

[30] The described application of correlations to a Monte Carlo simulation refers to the method that is employed by the author in 'RiskMaster' and 'RiskEase' to deal with the correlation problem.

illustrated in Figure 44.

Figure 44 - Simulation model

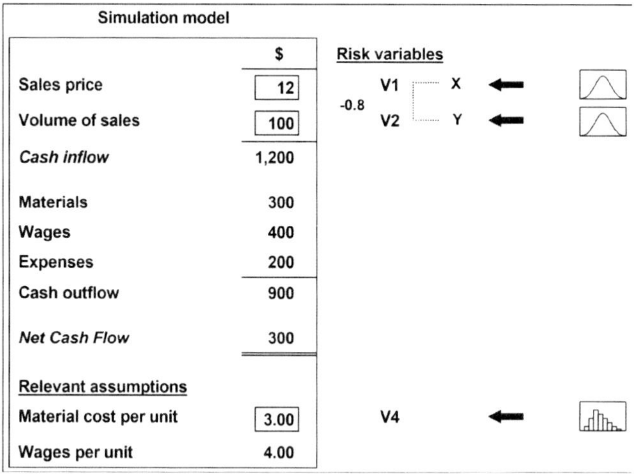

The scatter diagram in Figure 45 plots the sets of values generated during a simulation (200 runs) of our simple for two correlated variables (Sales price and Volume of sales). The simulation model included a condition for negative correlation and a correlation coefficient of -0.8. The range limits of values possible for the independent variable (sales price) were set at 8 to 16 and for the dependent variable (volume of sales) at 70 to 130[31]. Thus, the intercept and the slope of the regression line are:

$$a \text{ (intercept)} = 130$$

$$b \text{ (slope)} = \frac{(130 - 70)}{(16 - 8)} = -7.5$$

where:

a is the maximum Y value because the relationship is negative
b is expressed as a negative number because the relationship between the two variables is negative.

[31] It is assumed that the likelihood of occurrence of values within the defined range limits for the two variables is described by a normal probability distribution.

Figure 45 - Scatter diagram

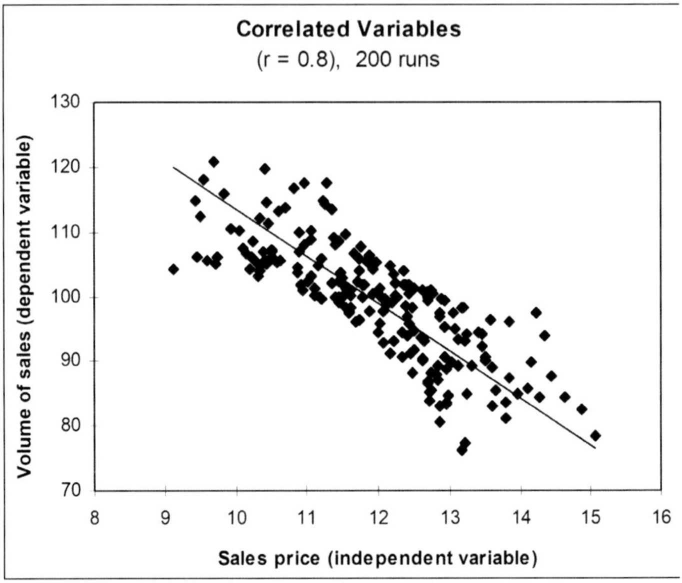

Simulation runs

The simulation runs stage is the part of the risk analysis process in which the computer takes over. Once all the assumptions, including correlation conditions, have been set it only remains to process the model repeatedly (each re-calculation is one run) until enough results are gathered to make up a representative sample of the near infinite number of combinations possible. A sample size of between 200 and 500 simulation runs should be sufficient in achieving this.

During a simulation the values of the "risk variables" are selected randomly within the specified ranges and in accordance with the set probability distributions and correlation conditions. The results of the model (that is the net present value of the project, the internal rate of return or in our simple example the "Net Cash Flow") are thus computed and stored following each run. This is illustrated in Figure 46 in which simulation runs are represented as successive frames of the model. Except by coincidence, each run generates a different result because the input values for the risk variables are selected randomly from their assigned probability distributions. The result of each run is calculated and stored away for statistical analysis (the final stage of risk analysis).

Figure 46 - Simulation runs

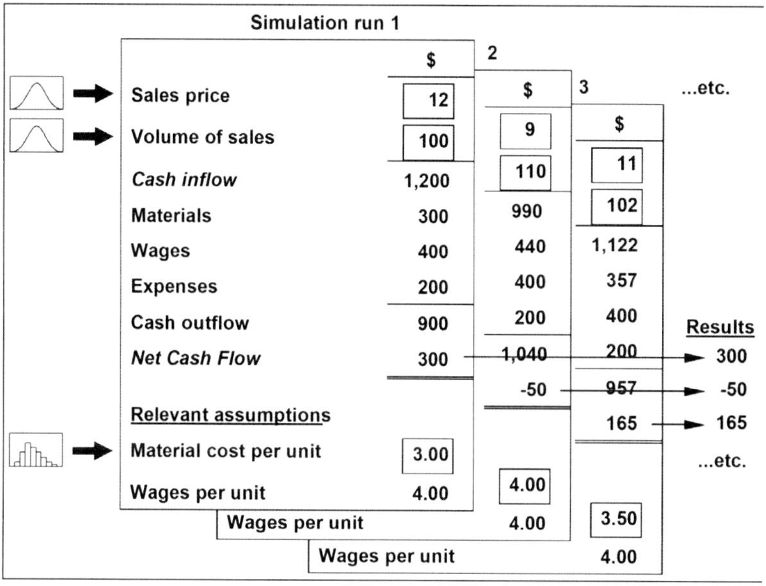

Analysis of results

The final stage in the risk analysis process is the analysis and interpretation of the results collected during the simulation runs stage. Every run represents a probability of occurrence equal to:

$$p = \frac{1}{n}$$

Where:

p	=	probability weight for a single run
n	=	sample size

Hence, the probability of the project result being below a certain value is simply the number of results having a lower value times the probability weight of one run[32]. By sorting the data in ascending order, it becomes

[32] For example, if 400 runs were generated then the probability weight is 1/400=0.0025. If 100 runs have an NPV of less than 0 then the probability for negative NPV is 100 x 0.0025=25%.

possible to plot the cumulative probability distribution of all possible results. Through this, one can observe the degree of probability that may be expected for the result of the project being above or below any given value. Project risk is thus portrayed in the position and shape of the cumulative probability distribution of project returns.

Figure 47 plots the results of our simple example following a simulation process involving 200 runs. The probability of making a loss from this venture is only about 10%.

Figure 47 - Distribution of results (net cash flow)

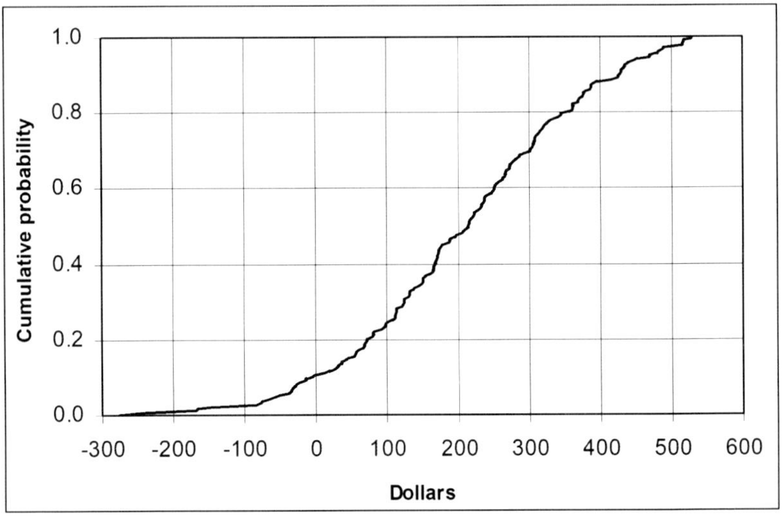

It is sometimes useful to compare the risk profiles of an investment from various perspectives. In Figure 48 the results of risk analysis, showing the cumulative probability distribution of net present values for the banker, owner and economy view of a certain project, are compared. The probability of having a net present value below zero for the economy's view case is nearly 0.4, while for that of the owner is less than 0.2. From the banker's view (or total investment perspective) the project seems quite safe as there seems to be about 95% probability that it will generate a positive NPV[33].

[33] An investment project can be evaluated from different view-points. In a financial appraisal the main difference between the Banker and Owner view is that the latter includes the financial flows from loan financing (loans are taken as cash inflow and

Figure 48 - Net present value distribution (from different project perspectives)

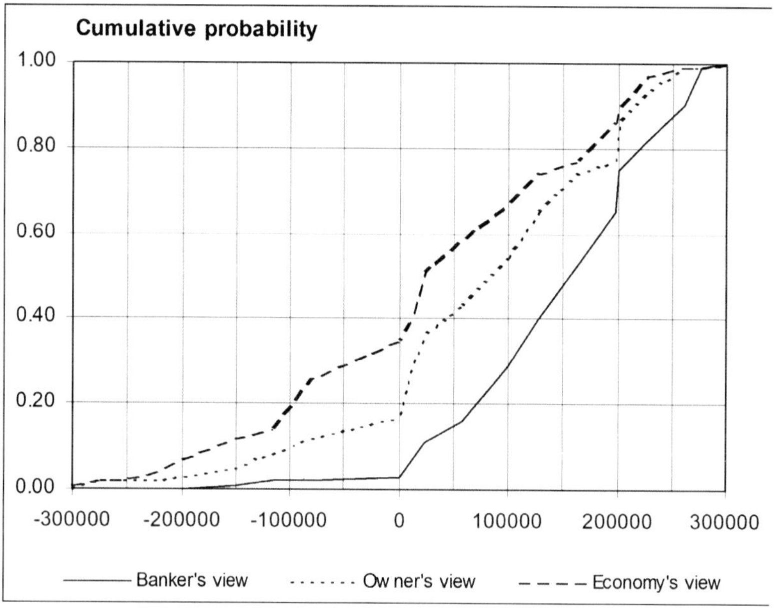

Interpreting the Results of Risk Analysis

The raw product of a risk analysis is a series of results which are organised and presented in the form of a probability distribution of the possible outcomes of the project. This by itself is a very useful picture of the risk/return profile of the project which can enhance the investment decision. However, the results of risk analysis raise some interpretation issues as regards the use of the net present value criterion. They also make possible various other measures of risk which further extend the usefulness of risk analysis in investment appraisal.

---

payments of interest and principal as cash outflow). From the economy's perspective one uses economic rather than financial prices adjusting for taxes and subsidies and excludes loans because they do not represent real resources. For a clear exposition of investment appraisal from different perspectives see Jenkins and Harberger (1991, pages.3:10-3:20).

Investment decision criteria

The basic decision rule for a project appraisal using certainty equivalent values as inputs and discounted at a rate adjusted for risk is simply to accept or reject the project depending on whether its NPV is positive or negative, respectively. Similarly, when choosing among alternative (mutually exclusive) projects, the decision rule is to select the one with the highest NPV, if it is positive. Investment criteria for a distribution of NPVs generated through the application of risk analysis are not always as clear-cut as this. We will look at two basic issues which have to do with risk analysis when used in conjunction with the NPV criterion: the choice of discount rate and the use of decision criteria.

The discount rate and the risk premium

In deterministic appraisal project risk is usually accounted for by including a risk premium in the discount rate which is used to appraise the project. The magnitude of this risk premium is basically the difference between the return usually required by investors undertaking similar projects and the risk-free interest rate. The derivation of the risk premium, particularly in countries with under-developed capital markets, is subjective and, often, rather arbitrary. Brealy and Myers (R. Brealy and S. Myers 1991, page 228) have argued that the most appropriate discount rate to use in a project appraisal subjected to risk analysis is the risk-free interest rate because any other discount rate would "pre-judge [the level of] risk" in a project. Another school of thought maintains that the discount rate should include a premium for systematic (or market) risk but not for unsystematic (or project) risk.

It is not the purpose of this paper to analyse and discuss the various schools of thought on the subject. Nevertheless, the author believes that the most appropriate discount rate is the one used in the deterministic appraisal. With the application of risk analysis and the careful consideration of the risk component of the main variables of a project and their relationship, it may be possible to establish a sounder basis on which to evaluate project risk. However, being able to appreciate the level and pattern of risk involved in a project does not, by itself, mean that we can also eliminate or even reduce project risk[34]. Nor does it mean that the project looks any less (or more)

[34] It is of course possible to reduce risk through project re-formulation and/or to reallocate it through the design of special contracts between various parties who may be better able to absorb or deal with certain types of risk. Indeed, this is one of the

risky to the outside world. The risk-free rate would therefore be most inappropriate because it would set a standard for the project which is below normal. The level of return, or hurdle, that the project is required to overcome to be considered worthwhile does not change simply because, as a result of risk analysis or any other tool, the investor gains a better sense of what constitutes project risk. After all, one does not change the discount rate when sensitivity or scenario analysis is applied. Risk analysis using the Monte Carlo method is fundamentally no different from scenario analysis. The only difference is that (based on the user's assumptions) the computer, rather than the analyst, builds the scenarios generated in the analysis.

Decision criteria

By using a discount rate that allows for risk, investment decision criteria normally used in deterministic analysis maintain their validity and comparability. The expected value of the probability distribution of NPVs (see Measures of risk below) generated using the same discount rate as the one used in conventional appraisal is a summary indicator of the project worth which is directly comparable (and should indeed be similar to) the NPV figure arrived at in the deterministic appraisal of the same project. Through the expected value of the NPV distribution therefore the decision criteria of investment appraisal still maintain their applicability.

However, because risk analysis presents the decision maker with an additional aspect of the project - the risk/return profile - the investment decision may be revised accordingly. The final decision is therefore subjective and rests largely on the investor's attitudes towards risk.

The general rule is to choose the project with the probability distribution of return that best suits one's own personal predisposition towards risk. The "risk-lover" will most likely choose to invest in projects with relatively high return, showing less concern in the risk involved. The "risk-averter" will most likely choose to invest in projects with relatively modest but rather safe returns.

However, assuming "rational" behaviour on behalf of the decision maker the following cases may be examined. Cases 1, 2 and 3 involve the decision criterion to invest in a single project. Cases 4 and 5 relate to investment decision criteria for choosing between alternative (mutually exclusive) projects.

---

most promising areas in which a risk analysis tool can be of tremendous value. See, for example, Lessard (1988) or Glenday (1989).

In every case examined both the cumulative and non-cumulative probability distributions are illustrated for comparison purposes. The cumulative probability distribution of the project returns is more useful for decisions involving alternative projects while the non-cumulative distribution is better for indicating the mode of the distribution and for understanding concepts related to expected value.

Case 1: The minimum point of the probability distribution of project return is higher than zero NPV (Figure 49).

Figure 49 - Case 1: Probability of negative NPV=0

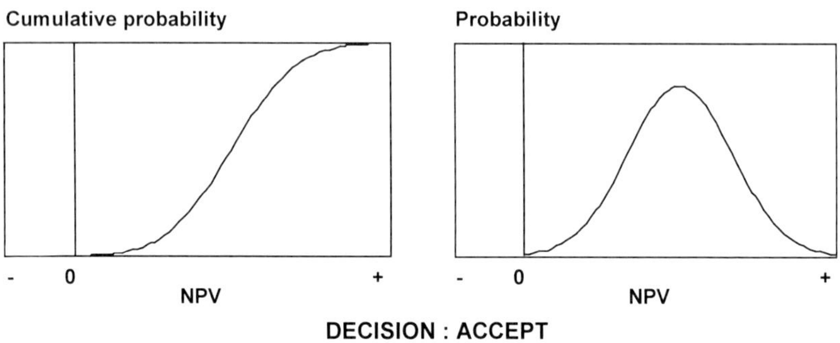

Since the project shows a positive NPV even under the "worst" of cases (i.e., no probability for negative return) then clearly the project should be accepted.

Case 2: The maximum point of the probability distribution of project return is lower than zero NPV (Figure 50).

Since the project shows a negative NPV even under the "best" of cases (no probability for positive return) then clearly the project should be rejected.

Case 3: The maximum point of the probability distribution of project return is higher and the minimum point is lower than zero Net Present Value (the curve intersects the point of zero NPV - Figure 51).

The project shows some probability of being positive as well as some probability of being negative; therefore, the decision rests on the risk predisposition of the investor.

Figure 50 - Case 2: Probability of positive NPV=0

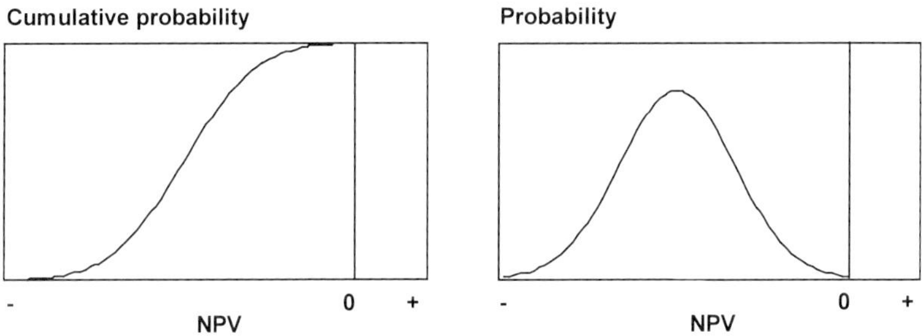

DECISION : REJECT

Figure 51 - Case 3: Probability of NPV greater than 0 and less than 1

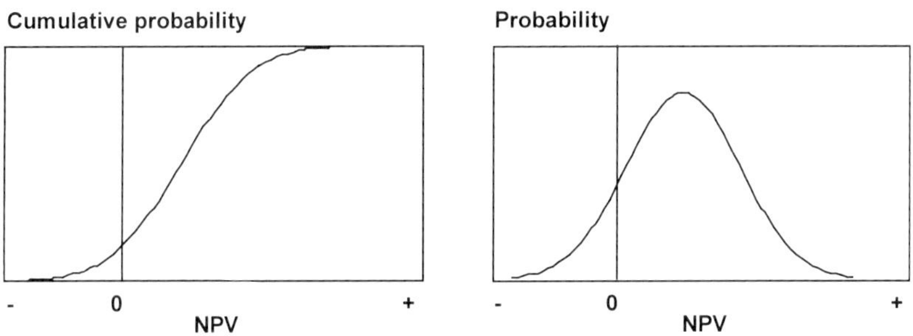

DECISION : INDETERMINATE

Case 4: Non-intersecting cumulative probability distributions of project return for mutually exclusive projects (Figure 52).

Figure 52 - Case 4: Mutually exclusive projects - non-intersecting curves

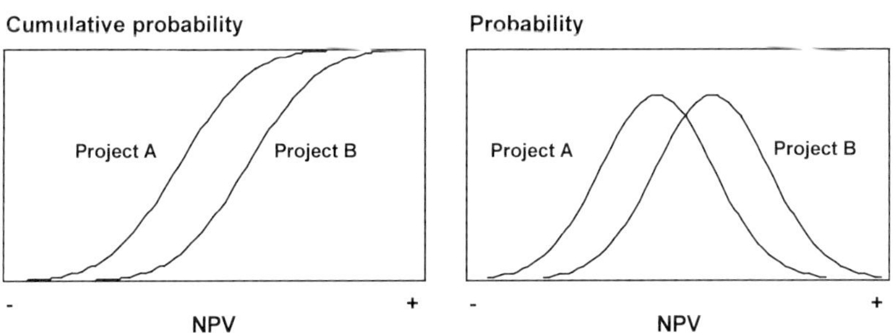

DECISION : CHOOSE PROJECT B

(given the same probability, one project always shows a higher return)

Given the same probability, the return of project B is always higher than the return of project A. Alternatively, given one particular return, the probability that it will be achieved or exceeded is always higher by project B than it is by project A. Therefore, we can deduce the first rule for choosing between alternative projects with risk analysis as:

Rule 1: If the cumulative probability distributions of the return of two mutually exclusive projects do not intersect at any point then always choose the project whose probability distribution curve is farther to the right.

Case 5: Intersecting cumulative probability distributions of project return for mutually exclusive projects (Figure 53).

Risk "lovers" will be attracted by the possibility of higher return and therefore will be inclined to choose project A. Risk "averters" will be attracted by the possibility of low loss and will therefore be inclined to choose project B.

Rule 2: If the cumulative probability distributions of the return of two mutually exclusive projects intersect at any point then the decision rests on the risk predisposition of the investor.

Figure 53 - Case 5: Mutually exclusive projects - intersecting curves

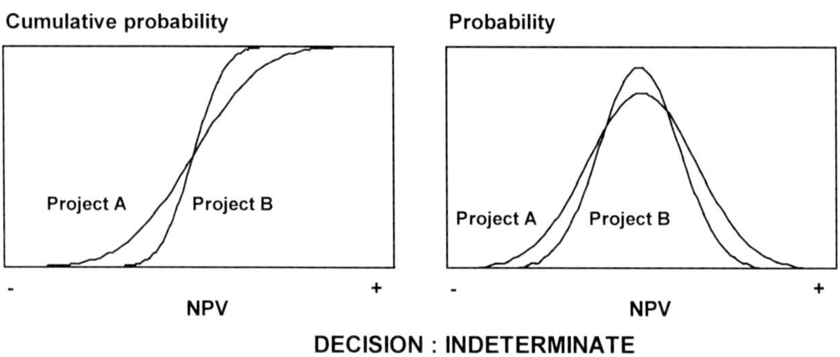

(high return versus low loss)

(Note: With non-cumulative probability distributions a true intersection is harder to detect because probability is represented spatially by the total area under each curve.)

Measures of risk

The results of a risk analysis application lend themselves to further analysis and interpretation using a series of measures which are based on the concept of expected value.

Expected value

The expected value statistic summarises the information contained within a probability distribution. It is a weighted average of the values of all the probable outcomes. The weights are the probabilities attached to each possible outcome. In risk analysis as applied in project appraisal the expected value is the sum of the products of the generated project returns and their respective probabilities[35]. This is illustrated in the simple example of a project with four possible returns and probabilities:

Table 4 - Expected Value calculation

Return		Probability		Expected Value
-10	x	0.2	=	-2.0
-5	x	0.3	=	-1.5
10	x	0.4	=	4.0
15	x	0.1	=	1.5
Total				2.0

The expected value of a project following a simulation is illustrated in Table 1. The total of all the negative returns times their respective probability is the expected loss from the project. In the above example this amounts to -3.5 (which is the sum of the "probability weighted" negative returns). The total of all the positive returns times their respective probability is the expected gain from the project. In the above example this amounts to 5.5 (which is the sum of the "probability weighted" positive returns). The expected value is, of course, the total of expected gain and expected loss.

The expected value statistic aggregates into a single number all the information that is depicted in a multi-valued probability distribution. Being a summary measure is therefore only a gross indicator of a project's worth. Measures of risk that employ expected value concepts are the "cost of uncertainty", the "expected loss ratio" and the "coefficient of variation"

[35] If the simulation process generated only unique results, then the probability weights would be the same for all possible outcomes (1 divided by sample size - see Analysis of results above).

which it is also used to analyse risk under conditions of limited liability.

Cost of uncertainty

The cost of uncertainty, or the value of information as it is sometimes called, is a useful concept that helps determine the maximum amount of money one should be prepared to pay to obtain information to reduce project uncertainty. This may be defined as the expected value of the possible gains foregone following a decision to reject a project, or the expected value of the losses that may be incurred following a decision to accept a project.

The expected gain forgone from rejecting a project is illustrated in the right-hand diagram of Figure 54 by the sum of the possible positive NPVs weighted by their respective probabilities. Similarly, the expected loss from accepting a project, indicated in the left-hand diagram, is the sum of all the possible negative NPVs weighted by their respective probabilities.

By being able to estimate the expected benefit that is likely to result from the purchase of more information, one can decide on whether it is worthwhile to postpone a decision to accept or reject a project and seek further information or whether to make the decision immediately. As a rule, one should postpone the investment decision if the possible reduction in the cost of uncertainty is greater than the cost of securing more information (including foregone profits if the project is delayed).

Figure 54 - Cost of uncertainty

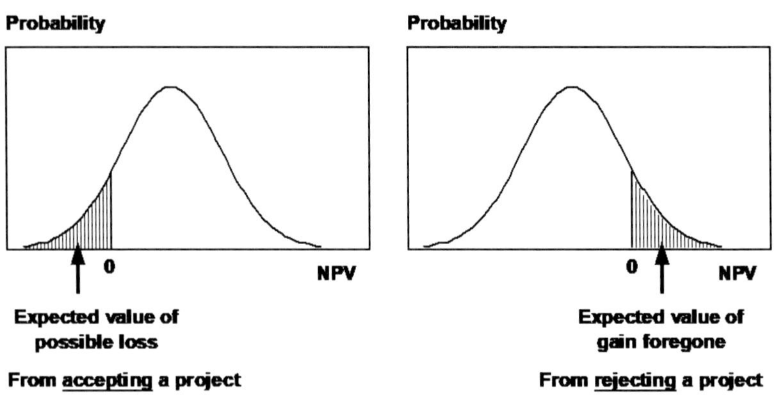

Expected loss ratio

The expected loss ratio (*el*) is a measure indicating the magnitude of expected loss relative to the project's overall expected NPV. This is expressed in the formula absolute value of expected loss divided by the sum of expected gain and absolute value of expected loss:

$$el = \frac{|\text{Expected Loss}|}{\text{Expected Gain} + |\text{Expected Loss}|}$$

It can vary from 0, meaning no expected loss, to 1, which means no expected gain. Diagrammatically, this is the probability weighted return derived from the shaded area to the left of zero NPV divided by the probability weighted return derived from the total distribution whereby the negative returns are taken as positive (see Figure 39).

A project with a probability distribution of returns totally above the zero NPV mark would compute an *el* value of 0, meaning that the project is completely unexposed to risk. On the other hand, a project with a probability distribution of returns completely below the zero NPV mark would result in an *el* of 1, meaning that the project is totally exposed to risk.

The ratio does not therefore distinguish between levels of risk for totally positive or totally negative distributions. However, within these two extreme boundaries the *el* ratio could be a useful measure for summarising the level of risk to which a project may be subjected. In the above example, the expected loss ratio is 3.5 / (5.5 + 3.5) or about 0.39.

Other methods for determining the risk exposure of a project's probability distribution of returns are possible. Such measures would vary depending on how one defines risk and, on the emphasis, one places on its major components. The *el* ratio is offered as an example of how one can use the results of risk analysis to assess and summarise the risk inherent in a project (illustrated in Figure 55). The *el* ratio defines risk to be a factor of both the shape and the position of the probability distribution of returns in relation to the "cut-off" mark of zero NPV.

Figure 55 - Expected loss ratio

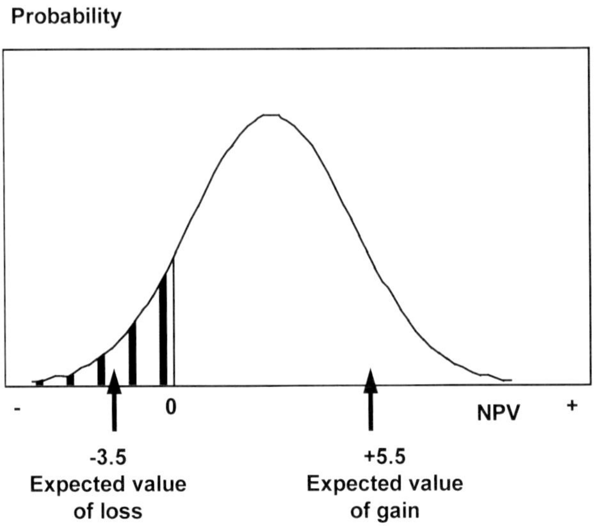

Coefficient of variation

The coefficient of variation is also a useful summary measure of project risk. It is the standard deviation of the projected returns divided by the expected value. Assuming a positive expected value, the lower the coefficient of variation the less the project risk.

Conditions of limited liability

The extent of maximum loss possible under conditions of limited liability is usually defined by the legal agreements entered by the various parties involved in a project. Looking at the investment in terms of present value the equity holders cannot lose more than the present value of their equity capital, the debt holders can only lose the present value of their loan capital, the creditors the present value of the extended credit and so on.

Consider the probability distribution of the return of a project as depicted in Figure 56.

Figure 56 - Risk under conditions of limited liability

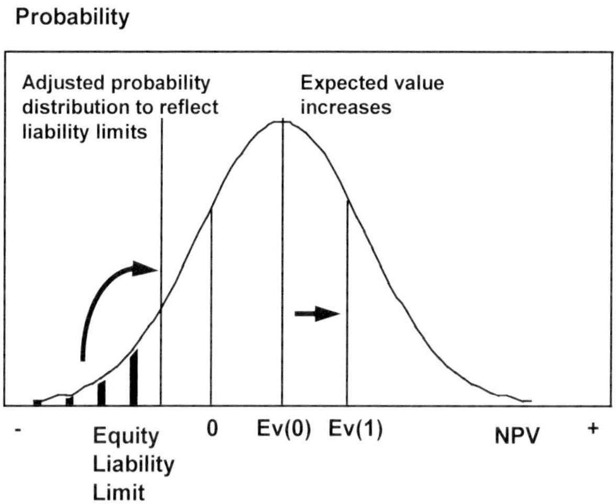

From the equity holders' point of view the tail of the distribution, which is beyond their maximum liability limit as defined by the present value of equity capital invested in the project, is not relevant. The probability of the project for generating a return lower than their maximum liability limit is therefore reassigned to the point of equity liability limit as shown in the diagram. This adjustment also has the effect of raising the expected value of the project from the point of view of the equity holders, from Ev(0) to Ev(1)[36].

Conclusion

Risk analysis is a useful tool extending the depth of project appraisal and enhancing the investment decision. Having practised the technique for several years the author can report the following specific advantages for risk analysis:

1. It enhances decision making on marginal projects. A project with a low single-value NPV may still be accepted following risk analysis on the grounds that its overall chances for yielding a satisfactory return are greater than is the probability of making an unacceptable

[36] This type of analysis may be useful in underlining the relative risk position of particular parties involved in a project.

loss. Likewise, a marginally positive project could be rejected based on being excessively risky, or one with a lower NPV may be preferred to another with a higher NPV because of a better risk/return profile.

2. It screens new project ideas and aids the identification of investment opportunities. Very often a new project concept is formulated that needs to be developed into a business opportunity. Before any real expenses are incurred to gather information for a full feasibility study it is possible to apply risk analysis widening the margins of uncertainty for the key project variables to reflect the lack of data. A substantial investment of human and financial resources is not incurred until the potential investors are satisfied that the preliminary risk/return profile of the project seems to be acceptable.
3. It highlights project areas that need further investigation and guides the collection of information. Risk analysis can contain the costs of investigation and fieldwork aiming at improving the accuracy of a forecast relating to particular project variables. If the cost for obtaining such information is greater than the expected benefit likely to result from the purchase of the information (see the Cost of uncertainty above), then the expense is not justified.
4. It aids the reformulation of projects to suit the attitudes and requirements of the investor. A project may be redesigned to take account for the particular risk predispositions of the investor.
5. It induces the careful re-examination of the single-value estimates in the deterministic appraisal. The difficulty in specifying range limits and probability distributions for risk analysis often resides in the fact that the projected values are not adequately researched. The need to define and support explicit assumptions in the application of risk analysis therefore forces the analyst to also critically review and revise the base-case scenario.
6. It helps reduce project evaluation bias through eliminating the need to resort to conservative estimates as a means of reflecting the analyst's risk expectations and predispositions.
7. It facilitates the thorough use of experts who usually prefer to express their expertise in terms of a probability distribution rather than having to compress and confine their opinion in a single value.
8. It bridges the communication gap between the analyst and the decision maker. The execution of risk analysis in a project appraisal involves the collection of information which to a large part reflects the acquired knowledge and expertise of top executives in an organisation. By getting the people who have the responsibility of

accepting or rejecting a project to agree on the ranges and probability distributions used in risk analysis the analyst finds an invaluable communication channel through which the major issues are identified and resolved. The decision maker in turn welcomes his involvement in the risk analysis process as he recognises it to be an important management decision role which also improves his/her overall understanding of the appraisal method.

9. It supplies a framework for evaluating project result estimates. Unlike the prediction of deterministic appraisal which is almost always refuted by the actual project result, the probabilistic approach is a methodology which facilitates empirical testing.
10. It provides the necessary information base to facilitate a more efficient allocation and management of risk among various parties involved in a project. Once the various sources of risk have been assessed, project risk may be contractually allocated to those parties who are best able to bear it and/or manage it. Moreover, it enables the testing of possible contractual arrangements for the sale of the products or the purchase of project inputs between various parties until a satisfactory formulation of the project is achieved.
11. It makes possible the identification and measurement of explicit liquidity and repayment problems in terms of time and probability that these may occur during the life of the project. This becomes possible if the net-cash flow figures or other indicators of solvency included in a project appraisal model (for instance the debt service coverage ratio for each year) are monitored during the simulation process.

Finally, two words of caution:

- Overlooking significant inter-relationships among the projected variables can distort the results of risk analysis and lead to misleading conclusions. The analyst should take due care to identify the major correlated variables and to adequately provide for the impact of such correlations in the simulation.
- Risk analysis amplifies the predictive ability of sound models of reality. The accuracy of its predictions therefore can only be as good as the predictive capacity of the model employed.

V. Risk and Return Revisited

This chapter is based on the article "Risk Through the Looking Glass – The Pursuit of a return without the risk" published by Published by Savvides, S., ***World Economics***, Vol. 23, No. 4, October–December 2022

An alternate world of risk and return

The term "through the looking glass" is borrowed from Lewis Carroll's (1872) book where Alice's pet cat begins to wonder what the world is like on the other side of a mirror with the reflected scene displayed on its surface. To her surprise, she was able to pass through the glass to experience the *alternate world* on the other side. This describes rather well the *alternate world of risk and return* following the so-called *liberalisation of financial markets* which carried the world through such a mirror.

The myth of the risk-free return is because of a widespread fallacy of what constitutes an *investment* and what risk is really. An investment can only be referring to capital that is funding a project in the real economy and which creates wealth and hence earns a return to equity. There is no return without a risk therefore in a productive (wealth adding) venture. There is always some risk that a capital investment project or a business undertaking will fail to attain a desired or required return. This is a fact of life, but it is also what drives the real economy.

Risk and return are like two sides of a coin. There is no way in a free and openly competitive economy that one can detach risk from the return. It is of course possible sometimes to reduce risk by better formulating a business venture as it is also probable, in some cases, for certain stakeholders in a project to enjoy the return while passing on the risk to other parties. But ***risk cannot be eliminated completely*** from a capital investment in the real economy. The only way to eliminate risk is found not in wealth creation projects but rather in wealth extraction deals that invariably involve the transfer of existing assets.

The fable and promise of a return without the risk emanates from the wrong use of the word ***investment*** which is used inadvertently and loosely by many to describe funding of mostly non-productive uses. Such as it is, for example, the issue and sale of bonds on asset backed rents in the Finance,

Real Estate and Insurance sector (better known as FIRE). Hedge funds and investment banks serve such promise to their clients when they create special bond funds that they then use to purchase asset-backed securities that extract rents from existing assets.

Funding the acquisition of existing rentier assets however is not a capital investment. It does not create or add anything to the real economy. It simply transfers the assets and rights emanating from such acquisition from one party to another. There is a profit or loss emanating to both sides as with all else. But it does not constitute a real capital investment. It is merely the use of funding to earn some income, usually through rents, to the participants of such schemes or funds while not putting their wealth at risk. Such earnings do not come from a new business venture. The so called "investment" in essence is simply the funding by which an existing asset is acquired. The economy does not get wealthier because existing wealth changes hands. It simply means that the profits (or losses) are now accruing to different beneficiaries.

The term risk-free is rather loosely used in financial markets and in essence refers only to what assets can be acquired and the fund can have earnings from with limited risk. It is not a capital investment in the real economy which, by comparison, creates new wealth. It is rather in reference to what one can earn through some sort of asset-backed rentier income. But even that is rarely entirely risk-free as there is no guarantee that one would not default or that inflation may not take away any real earnings from such owning such assets.

Moreover, the pursuit of a "return without the risk" is causing the banking system to lose its direction and Governments to become complicit to a systemic conspiracy against the welfare of the people whose interests their elected representatives in a democracy are supposed to be protecting and serving. And it is based on an erroneous concept of *what risk really is.*

What is really risk

In investment and finance theory, "Risk" refers to the **volatility** of expected return. In the context of capital investment appraisal **risk** may be defined as ***the possible negative outcomes times the probability of occurrence*** with respect of the projected return (Net Present Value). Or what is termed as the **Expected Loss** of a probability distribution after applying risk analysis to a model using Monte Carlo simulation methodology.

Figure 57 - Upside Volatility is not Risk

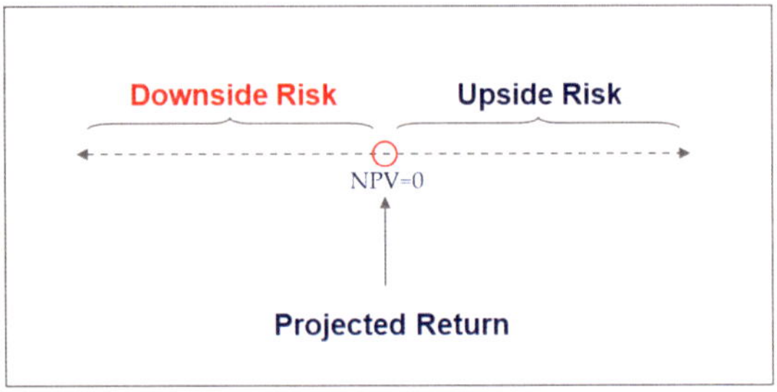

In investment and finance theory, the term and concept of risk refers strictly to the volatility of expected return. This has been largely established by what is known as the Capital Asset Pricing Model, proposed by a number of Nobel winning economists including Sharpe (1964), Markowitz (1999) and others.

The Capital Asset Pricing Model (CAPM) is a model that describes the relationship between the expected return and the risk of investing in stocks and securities. It argues that the expected return on a security is equal to the risk-free return plus a risk premium, which is based on the beta of that security. Risk and return from the vantage point of the floor of a Stock exchange which is in the main speculative is also based on a concept whereby risk is perceived as volatility of return. This however is not strictly speaking correct. Upside volatility is not really risk. Higher than expected returns are not risk. Moreover, there is no return without risk in the real economy. Even the risk-free return that that the CAPM model is based on is not really without risk. And in most cases where this is sought it is not even an investment as it creates nothing.

Volatility is already factored into the discount rate used to calculate the Net Present Value. The higher the Volatility the higher the Expected Return. Not all volatility however is really risk. Volatility has a good side. People like it when it makes their returns go up. Hence to consider that any volatility (positive or negative) implies more risk is to say the least contrary to any logic. The Capital Asset Pricing Model methodology seems to have conveniently convinced most in the financial industry, including the academia, as it is basically argued the Market return is the optimum one can attain. Accepting this as a premise it follows that through a diversified portfolio of assets one can attain the reduction of risk as the overall return of such portfolio gradually optimises around something close to the market return.

Figure 58 - The Capital Asset Pricing Model (CAPM)

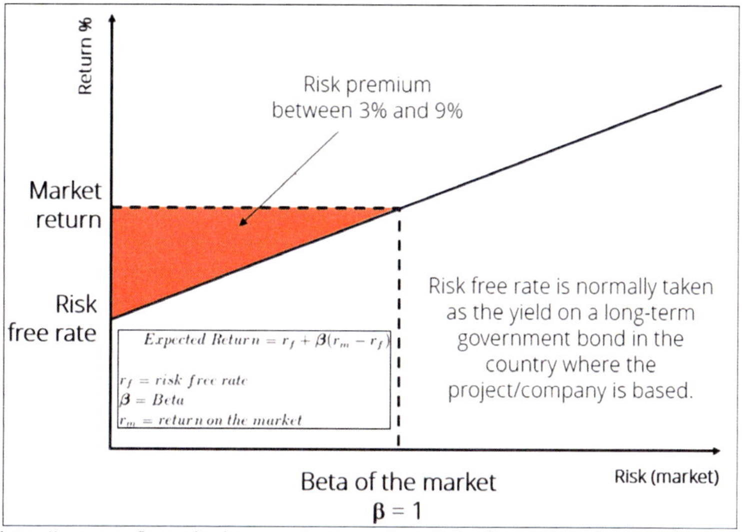

https://corporatefinanceinstitute.com/resources/knowledge/finance/what-is-capm-formula/

As illustrated in Figure 59 however not all volatility is risk. At least, not any volatility. In conventional thinking of what risk is the above returns may constitute a high-risk investment. This is contrary to any common-sense understanding of what constitutes risk. As it is illustrated in the example, where practically all outcomes are positive variations above the expected return.

Risk defined as expected loss

Moving on from using volatility of return to Expected Loss in probabilistic analysis (using Monte Carlo Simulation methodology) one can attach probabilities to all possible outcomes. It is therefore possible to distinguish between downside and upside risk. Whereby the upside are all the probability weighted outcomes above 0 NPV (the Expected Gain) and the downside where all the probability weighted negative NPV outcomes (the Expected Loss) constitutes really what depicts and summarises a project real risk.

Figure 59 - Upside volatility is not Risk[37]

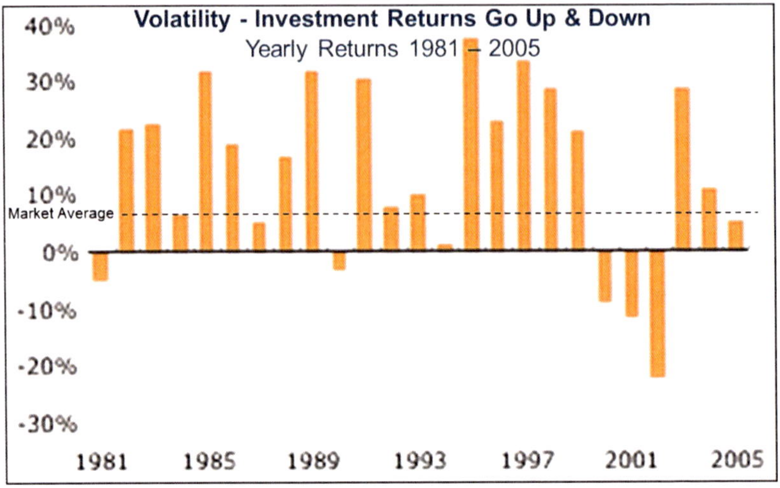

As it illustrated in Figure 60, in a Monte Carlo Simulation methodology risk analysis one defines probability distributions on the key risk variables in a financial model which is used to appraise a capital investment project. The simulation generates probability distributions of the outcomes (in our example the Net Present Value) given the expected range and probabilities defined for these risk variables. As a result, one can now have an idea of the spread of return possible including its likelihood of occurrence. On further analysis it is possible to estimate Expected Gain (positive) and Expected Loss (negative). The sum of the two always equals the Expected Value of the whole probability distribution of the outcome. Which can be defined as:

$$EV = \Sigma \text{ [Outcomes X Probability]}$$

Expected Return is therefore the sum of all probability weighted outcomes of a Monte Carlo Simulation[38]. With this available one can then distinguish

---

[37] Source: *S&P's Micropal. Graph shows annual returns for S&P 500 Index and assumes reinvestment of all dividends. Taken from Franklin Templeton Investments website on "Investment Risk".*

[38] *All Monte Carlo simulation and the analysis that follows, including the Risk Aversion Analysis referred to here, was done using RiskEase© by RiskEase Ltd at* www.riskease.com. *RiskEase was the application created by Savvakis Savvides (initially as RiskMaster and subsequently renamed to RiskEase) that was the*

and estimate risk where it really belongs. Only the negative outcomes in the case of Net Present Value or outcomes that fall below the expected return when another measure (such as the Internal Rate of Return) is used.

Figure 60 - Uncertainty of input variables drive volatility of return

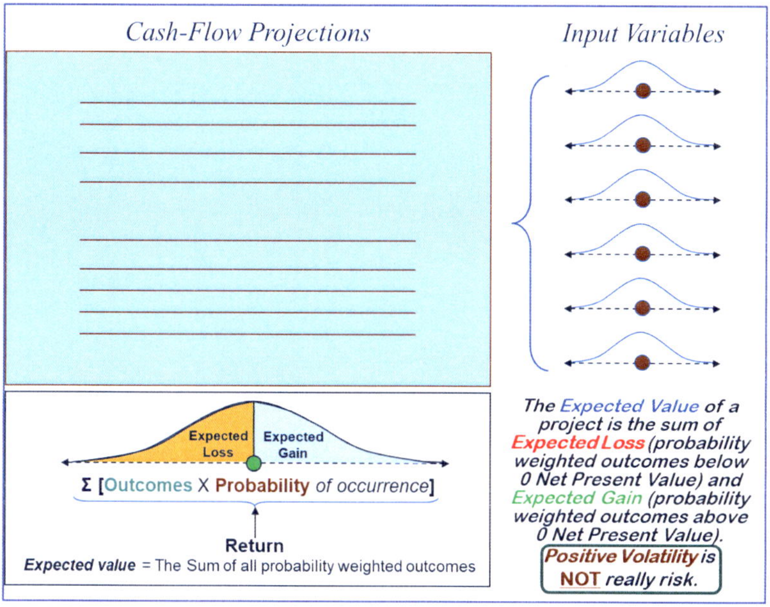

We are therefore able to progress from the overall variance/volatility assessment of risk to the Probabilistic assessment of risk through the estimation of Expected Loss, as illustrated in Figure 61. The diagram also illustrates an important attribute of investing in the real economy rather than following a hedged or low risk approach. The investment in the real economy in a project that creates new wealth is almost always a potentially higher risk investment. While it is possible to attain much higher returns in general it is also more likely that in some instances one may also lose more if the project fails. But in general, the average expected return on a real project vis-à-vis a limited or low risk positioning on asset-backed returns is higher. Of course, this means that the risk premium on the real economy project is also higher. But implicit in this analysis is also that investing in low risk (hedged risk) projects in effect lowers the potential performance of

---

companion software add-in to the very successful paper by the author of Risk Analysis in Investment Appraisal (Savvides 1994).

the economy in total.

Figure 61 - Expected Loss as measure of Risk

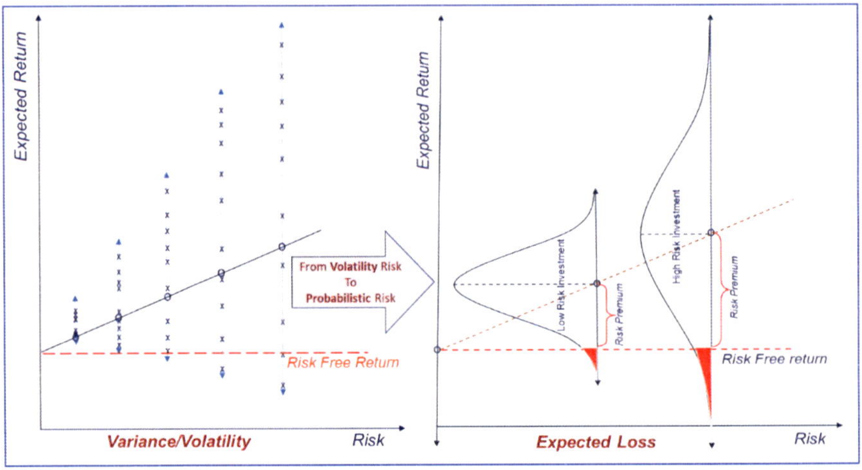

Risk aversion and the investment decision

In effect, the current money-managing investors weigh up the risk of losing money and increasing in weight as they become higher in the scale against the potential higher returns of a proposed capital investment. As an example, consider the project below which shows a positive Net Present Value of about €35 million. Given a risk neutral preference this project should be accepted (Figure 62).

However, if one applies the risk aversion bias of potential investors it is quite probable that it may be rejected. As the negative flows weigh heavier on the scale of risk aversion.

If one applies the risk aversion preferences of an investor (shown as an extended bend downwards on the Investor Risk Preference chart in figure 63 – left side box) then the Expected Loss as adjusted to take account of the investor's risk profile may turn a risk neutral decision from positive to a negative one (figure 63 - right side box).

Figure 62 - Expected Loss as measure of risk - Weighing up Expected Loss

Return	Prob	Expected Value	Expected Loss	Expected Gain
-150,000,000	0.0000	0	0	0
-132,500,000	0.0000	0	0	0
-115,000,000	0.0000	0	0	0
-97,500,000	0.0004	-39,000	-39,000	0
-80,000,000	0.0026	-208,000	-208,000	0
-62,500,000	0.0040	-250,000	-250,000	0
-45,000,000	0.0202	-909,000	-909,000	0
-27,500,000	0.0452	-1,243,000	-1,243,000	0
-10,000,000	0.0962	-962,000	-962,000	0
7,500,000	0.1394	1,045,500	0	1,045,500
25,000,000	0.1776	4,440,000	0	4,440,000
42,500,000	0.1836	7,803,000	0	7,803,000
60,000,000	0.1472	8,832,000	0	8,832,000
77,500,000	0.0986	7,641,500	0	7,641,500
95,000,000	0.0512	4,864,000	0	4,864,000
112,500,000	0.0204	2,295,000	0	2,295,000
130,000,000	0.0098	1,274,000	0	1,274,000
147,500,000	0.0032	472,000	0	472,000
165,000,000	0.0002	33,000	0	33,000
182,500,000	0.0002	36,500	0	36,500
200,000,000	0.0000	0	0	0
		35,125,500	-3,611,000	38,736,500

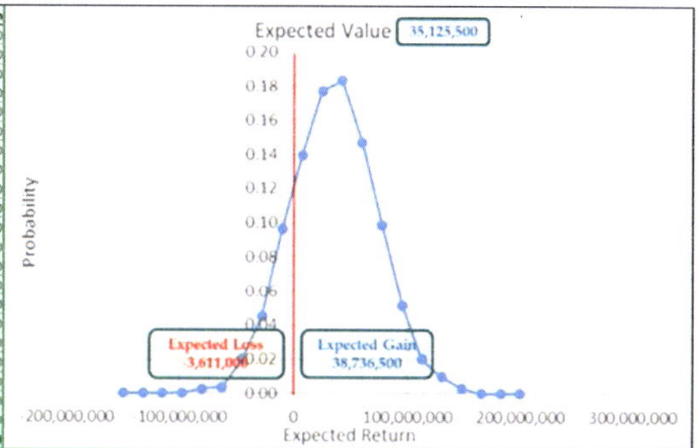

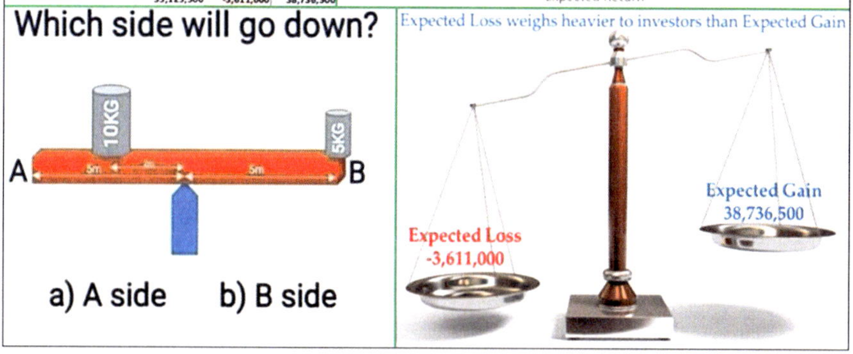

Figure 63 - Expected Loss adjusted for Risk Aversion

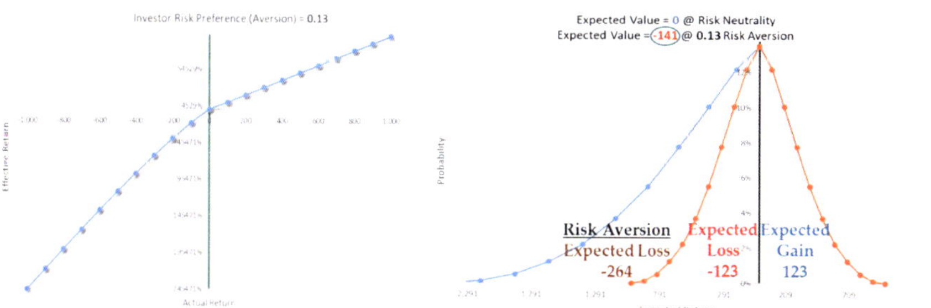

When the risk aversion preferences of investors are factored into the analysis a positive Net Present Value project may be rejected. As it is illustrated in the example in Figure 48 where the negative returns are adjusted to reflect the risk aversion preferences of a particular investor. In the example, the negative cash flows are multiplied by a "Risk Adjustment Factor" (RAF) to reflect the investor's risk aversion preferences. The positive cash flows remain unaffected. The probabilities also do not change as what is likely to happen is not affected by risk attitudes. The RAF is simply a linear adjustment of how negative cash flows may weigh on an investor's decision scale for a given project.

Risk aversion analysis can be applied to any probability distribution generated from a set of Monte Carlo Simulation results. Risk Aversion Analysis also allows one to use the Solver in Excel to optimise to find the exact RAF that adjusts the negative cash flows so that the Expected Value is equal a given Expected Return level[39]. As illustrated in Figure 64, in the case of Net Present Value the adjustment is the one that makes the Expected Value to be equal to 0 (RAF=1.138). The RAF is also an objective indicator of the capacity of a given investment to withstand risk aversion investor biases.

Figure 64 - When Expected Loss is adjusted to reflect risk aversion

NPV Owner		X 1.138	Expected Value adjusted for Investor Risk Preferences		
Return	Prob	Return adjusted for Risk	Expected Value (Utility)	EL(u)	EG(u)
-150,000,000	0.0000	-2,029,726,022	0	0	0
-132,500,000	0.0000	-1,762,410,891	0	0	0
-115,000,000	0.0000	-1,499,949,804	0	0	0
-97,500,000	0.0004	-1,242,977,108	-497,191	-497,191	0
-80,000,000	[illegible]	-992,339,503	-2,580,083	-2,580,083	0
-62,500,000	0.0040	-749,230,415	-2,996,922	-2,996,922	0
-45,000,000	0.0202	-515,473,848	-10,412,572	-10,412,572	0
-27,500,000	0.0452	-294,260,340	-13,300,567	-13,300,567	0
-10,000,000	0.0962	-93,026,670	-8,949,166	-8,949,166	0
7,500,000	0.1394	7,500,000	1,045,500	0	1,045,500
25,000,000	0.1776	25,000,000	4,440,000	0	4,440,000
42,500,000	0.1836	42,500,000	7,803,000	0	7,803,000
60,000,000	0.1472	60,000,000	8,832,000	0	8,832,000
77,500,000	0.0986	77,500,000	7,641,500	0	7,641,500
95,000,000	0.0512	95,000,000	4,864,000	0	4,864,000
112,500,000	0.0204	112,500,000	2,295,000	0	2,295,000
130,000,000	0.0098	130,000,000	1,274,000	0	1,274,000
147,500,000	0.0032	147,500,000	472,000	0	472,000
165,000,000	0.0002	165,000,000	33,000	0	33,000
182,500,000	0.0002	182,500,000	36,500	0	36,500
200,000,000	0.0000	200,000,000	0	0	0
		Risk Aversion Factor	0	-38,736,500	38,736,500

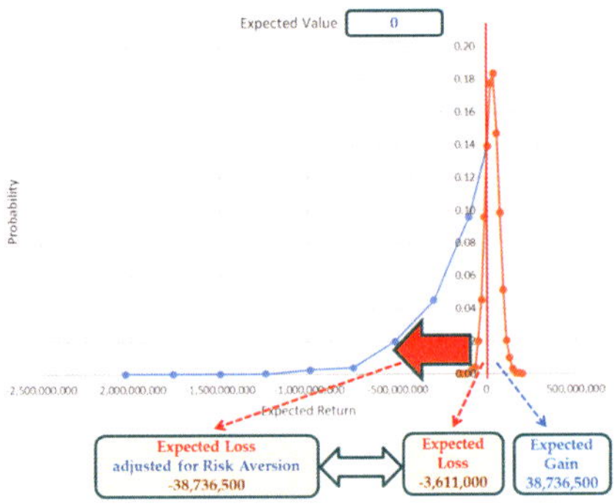

Risk aversion has a very significant impact on the real economy and in consequence to the general welfare of the people. As more and more capital investment projects in the real economy do not constitute the ideal investment for the risk averse preferences of wealthy investors (including hedge funds, investment banks, and wealth management arms of banks and so on). The overall impact of this extreme inequality is that through the elusive promise of a return without the risk offered by financial market "experts" (and as supported by the prevailing academic thinking), the bulk

[39] *The example has been done using the Risk Aversion Analysis module of RiskEase© software,* www.riskease.com.

of funding is directed towards rentier rather than productive uses. This causes a systemic disconnect of financing away from wealth creation and towards wealth extraction. Consequently, the real productive economy suffers and in effect slowly but surely the world becomes poorer.

Extreme inequality of income and wealth also increases risk aversion. This is to some extent to be expected since the natural concern of the very wealthy is to maintain what they have rather than to risk losing it in the real projects in the real productive economy. What they seek and look for therefore is to have a decent but safe return on the enormous wealth they have amassed. In the case of Pension or Insurance funds, because of the nature of their mandate, they cannot undertake but limited amounts of risk on the money they manage. The concentration of money in the hands of the very few therefore skews investor attitudes towards risk aversion. Moreover, there is a further reason for shying away from a real economy investment as they do not possess the skills, competence and understanding of such projects. It comes as no surprise therefore that in most cases they are unwilling to take on the risks inherent in the productive economy. By contrast, while entrepreneurs who master their trade see a new venture as a challenge, the very wealthy and huge money funds see such investments as potential black holes which can take them and their clients into an abyss.

The result of extreme inequality and the risk aversion preferences of the wealthy and special interest groups prevailing is that funding is directed away from economically productive investments and into low-risk investments (often bonds and asset-backed securities) that hedge the risk. With the reduction of volatility through such low-risk investments however also comes a lower expected return than the average expected return in projects in the real economy. Hence, the real economy underperforms, and general welfare overall suffers a loss (as illustrated in the Figure 65).

A banking system that facilitates wealth transfer

Every capital investment whether deemed to have negative or positive net present value has, like a coin, two sides. One is the return side and the other the risk side. Any attempt to detach one from the other almost always results in misallocation of economic resources where some benefit at the expense of those who are undertaking the risk. This is magnified by a world economy where there is huge concentration of wealth, and which is facilitated by a loose financial system that enables banks to create money and pass on the risk to their borrowers (Savvides 2020). This allows banks to pass on their loan assets to hedge funds and wealth managers with borrowers ending up

Figure 65 - Expected Return decreases the greater the inequality

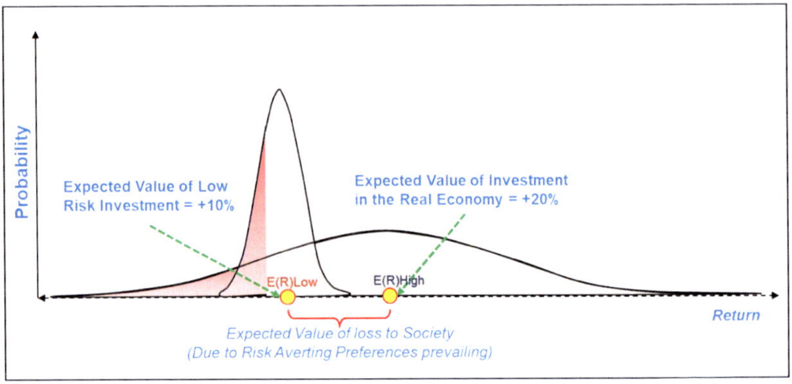

at the mercy of those who are looking to position "mountains" of money in assets with moderate return but with relatively low risk. Such risk/return profiles however can only be basically found in the transfer of existing assets rather than in the creation of new wealth through new viable capital investment projects. In this manner, and with the banking system conveniently acting as a facilitator, a huge transfer of wealth from the many to the few takes place which in turn exacerbates the concentration of wealth and the inequality problem[40].

The paradox of detaching the risk from return can be demonstrated in the expected value calculation which is the probability distribution of the expected outcome of a capital investment (Savvides 1994). This in turn has two aspects or sides which together make up the expected return. One is the *expected loss* which is composed of the likely instances where the expected return is below the required (such as 0 NPV) times the probability of occurrence for each instance and on the other side the *expected gain* which is made up of all the likely instances where it is expected to have a return above the required level (positive NPV) times the probability of occurrence of each instance. The expected loss ratio is the expected value of loss (or *Expected Loss*) in absolute terms divided by the sum of the expected value

[40] In addition, banks enjoy an indirect subsidy by legislation that allows interest on borrowings to be tax exempt (the tax shield). Banks have also been granted the right to create money out of thin air instead of that being the prerogative of the Sovereign. And in a huge paradox, sovereign governments now borrow at interest from the banks what they could have created themselves and even guarantee deposits and save the banks as and when is needed.

of gain (or *Expected Gain*) and the expected loss in absolute terms, as illustrated in Figure 66 (where the Expected Value of the project +2 is the sum of the Expected Loss and Expected Gain):

Figure 66 - Example of risk analysis results and Expected Value

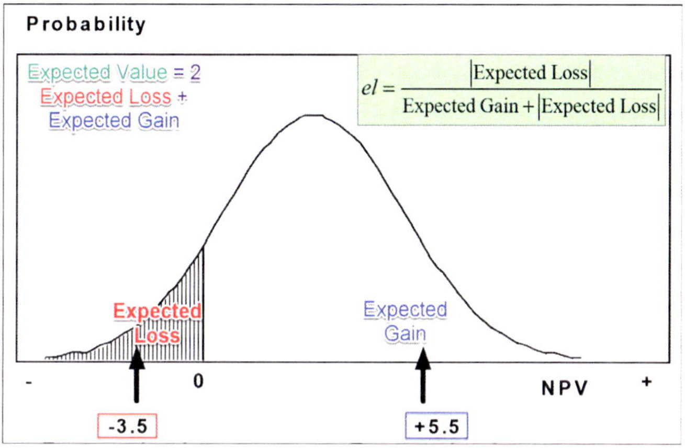

When an entrepreneur is funding a project out of own equity, he must decide whether he believes he can manage these risks and undertake the investment against the prospect to make a good expected return. This is how a normal laissez-faire economy works.

Now consider the situation, which is common today, whereby half, if not most of the capital investment, is funded through loans. If we assume that 50% of a project is loan financed how does the above change the risk-return situation? As far as the risk to the owner of the project is concerned, although the investors provide only 50% of the funding required, they undertake the whole of the risk by providing full recourse to the banks for the lending in terms of collaterals and guarantees. In other words, the lenders in effect undertake no real risk. And for that, the bank takes a reduced but relatively certain return in terms of the interest agreed and other bank charges. From there on, there are two possible outcomes for a lender. To collect its principal and interest or for the loan to become non-performing and thus to call it in and collect on the collateral and guarantees at hand.

The intriguing, but also rather worrying question, is what is more likely to happen, or may even be preferred by banks, in such cases where a loan becomes non-performing, and it needs to be recovered? Strange as it may seem, often, it is more likely that banks opt to sell a loan to funds or other wealth managers rather than executing whatever recourse they have at hand. This process however facilitates wealth extraction and wealth transfer from the distressed borrowers to the Funds or other third parties that are buying these (including substantial proceeds for intermediaries – such as investment banks and other advisors). Paradoxically, this systemic method seems to be serving those who control the banks and primarily its executives and major shareholders better than if the bank was to be granting only viable loans with a good repayment capability that do not become non-performing.

When one is fully covered as in the case of a bank, illustrated in the example in Figure 11, the expected loss part of an investment *does not apply*. In effect, this means that the expected value of an acquired project asset as it applies to the lender is in fact higher because of full recourse in the event of any losses. So, as in the simple example above, the expected value of the probability distribution for all intends and purposes is +5.5 for the perspective of the lender who can call on the securities and take over the assets of the borrower. But the paradox is that if a bank utilises these securities directly, the maximum compensation that can be attained is the principal of the loan plus any accrued interest. However, if a bank is allowed (or even encouraged by the system as it is the rule now) to sell the loan asset to a third party with all the collaterals and guarantees in place, it would be possible for all parties involved in such deals to extract more than just if the bank was to call in on the loan and manage the recovery process itself in the depth of time. The bank would still not show in its books any abnormal profits but in such deals the boundaries for many in its immediate and peripheral environment to gain from such deals are enormous and not always apparent or even transparent.

In today's environment banks seem to be making more money by granting loans that become non-performing rather than economically viable ones that support the productive economy. Black (2005) argues very convincingly that banks often seek and even encourage giving subprime (or liar's) loans. This is spurred by a massive and ever-growing demand for buying relatively risk-free assets albeit with some moderate but rather certain return, which happens to be the conservative risk/return profile sought by those who have amassed huge amounts of money and wealth.

Banking has evolved to perform this unsavoury role. Bankers seem to have totally lost focus of what always was, and still should be, their primary mission; that of productive lending that funds and fosters economic growth. With the so-called financial liberalisation, there emerged faster and easier

Figure 67 - Calculation of Expected Value using Monte Carlo Simulation

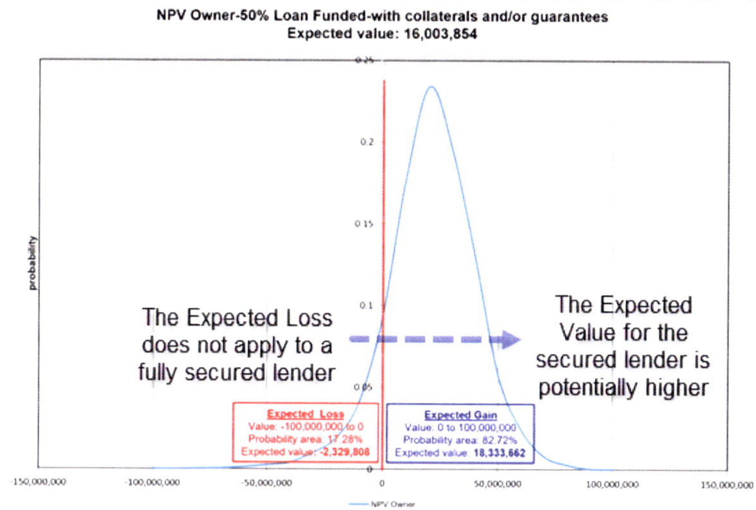

ways for those in control of banks to respond and facilitate the needs of the huge concentration of money in the world. But to tap such opportunities for quick and handsome profits a bank must grant far many more loans than the usual number of economically viable loans. There is no easy way to get to such vast portfolio of loans even if one was to apply proper assessment and good banking practices which, in the experience of the author, is as far from what happens nowadays as it ever was. Many of these loans end up as non-performing therefore which conveniently also enables the transfer of wealth to funds.

As it is demonstrated in Figure 68, it is the increasing inequality due to the concentration of money and power in the world and the deregulation though a loose financial and banking system that has brought the world at the brink of stagnation and a prolonged economic depression. Complicit in this *disconnect of funding from wealth creation* are many, including the regulatory authorities for banks, academia, rating agencies and last, but not least, politicians, Savvides (2021).

Figure 68 - Increasing inequality leads to wealth extraction

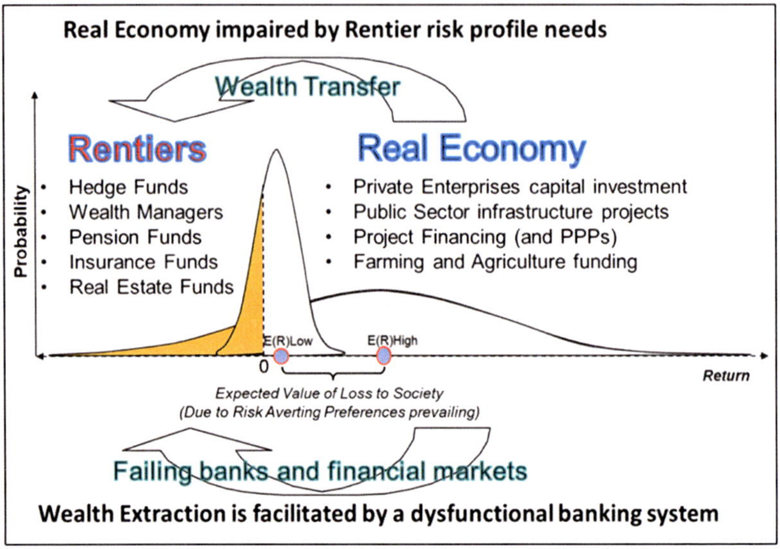

Risk and return driving economic development

Risk and return are the twin cylinders of the engine driving a free market economy. In the real economy, there is no such thing as a return without risk. Risk is simply the uncertainty that encompasses an entrepreneurial capital investment project as its future cash flows cannot be determined with certainty. Economic development is attained by taking on risks that are part and parcel of productive capital investments. Where the priority is to contain or even eliminate investment risk while attaining a good return, inevitably the end-result is not wealth creation but wealth extraction. This is because only in situations of forced wealth transfers can one hope to find such conditions of a return without the risk. These forced acquisitions of other people's assets serve only the "rentiers" rather than the productive sectors of the economy and inevitably result in increased inequality in the world. It is taxpayers that ultimately bear the cost of such forced acquisitions and transfers of wealth.

The original meaning of a free market, as discussed by classical political economists, was a market free from all forms of rent. By contrast, current economic thinking seems to be in the service of rentiers and financiers. It also almost completely neglects to consider the role of money and debt.

Economic policy is therefore formed using flawed economic models and leads to erroneous policies by governments and regulatory authorities around the world. This was a lesson learned in the Great Depression in the United States and led to the *Glass Steagall Act of 1933*, which separated commercial banking from investment banking. However, lobbying and pressure applied by special interests in Wall Street on the Clinton government led to the repeal of Glass Steagall and the introduction of the *Financial Services Modernization Act of 1999*. This let the genie out of the bottle, and it is now probably impossible to put it back in.

Economics is about using economic resources to maximise the utility (or welfare) of a society. To move an economy closer toward this goal it is necessary to employ capital and labour and other factors of production, such as land, as near as possible to their best and most efficient uses. However, the efficient employment of labour and other factors of production and the raising of the pace of economic development depends crucially on the productive employment of capital in funding economically viable projects in the real economy. This in effect means that a capital investment project, when appraised for the economy through cost-benefit analysis, should have a positive net present value (where the net cash flows of the project discounted at the opportunity cost of capital is higher than zero). It also follows that a viable investment should also be considered capable to service its debt.

Moreover, as with any new project the outcome is, by definition, uncertain it is also desirable to evaluate the impact of alternative possible scenarios considering the risks that are intrinsic to the project and consider whether the competence and capacity to overcome these is at hand. In other words, any new investment project should have a manageable risk profile and a decision on whether to undertake and provide the financing for it should depend on the outcome of such risk analysis.

Sustainable economic development therefore can only be attained if capital investment and financing is channelled towards funding the most viable and therefore also competitive projects. Real economic development comes from building on solid grounds and from funding projects which add net customer value and are cost effective. This holds true for both foreign and local investment projects. Only viable projects serve the cause of economic development. An investment which is likely to foreclose before its expected life span or which is likely to be unable to repay its loans only drags the economy even further into recession. This is a lesson the world should have learned by now as most of the loans that have been granted by banks in countries such as Cyprus, Ireland, Portugal, Italy and Spain in the past 20-30 years have become non-performing.

Current economic thinking does not distinguish between newly created and existing wealth. The reason is mainly because the Gross Domestic Product (GDP) of a nation is taken to be the total value added in a calendar year. In *The Wealth of Nations* Adam Smith described wealth as "the annual produce of the land and labour of the society". The emphasis on the word "produce" is the key to what wealth creation really is. It is about the creation of new wealth through productively combining the factors of production. Money has no intrinsic value and does not automatically create wealth. This only happens when money is used productively to fund new products and services which add real economic value (utility/consumer surplus) and thereby enhance economic and social welfare.

The world has however moved away from this fundamental premise of Economics. Even economists who were defending the existence of rentiers at the end of the 19th century could only do so on the premise that banks finance productivity. The writings of Adam Smith, Stuart Mill and Alfred Marshall led to the idea that economic resources should be directed towards industry instead of supporting landlords and the parasitic financial classes. The classical economists were arguing that rentiers were getting a free lunch, by extracting rather than creating wealth. Rentiers and neoclassical economists fought back by denying that economic rent was unearned. For example, John Bates Clarke argued that this income is a payment for the landlords' labour and enterprise and not, as J. S. Mill had characterised it, accruing "in their sleep". Interest was depicted as a payment for the "service" of lending productively, not as exploitation[41]. Defining and justifying interest as the "*earned payment for the service of lending productively*" was the moral justification for viewing banks as performing a vital economic role and in serving society. The departure from this fundamental premise is possibly the root cause of economic crises and the main reason why real economies are frequently in distress.

The gist of the debate about rentiers at the end of 19th and beginning or the 20th century, as it relates to banks, was whether banks provide a social service rather than extract rents. If banks lend only with respect of their own security considerations (guarantees and collaterals available) rather than by prudently assessing a project's (or a business') ability to repay, then debt can become wasteful and extractive. Such lending, if done in excess, leads

[41] Hudson (2018)

to financial bubbles and cause economic crises.

The deregulation of financial markets and the widely accepted misconception that structured assets and derivatives add to economic development have taken Economics "through the looking glass" and into an alternate world where the real economy has become weaker more unstable. The consequence of this is that money's vital role as a medium of exchange for goods and services has shifted towards one where it is now perceived as having its own intrinsic value causing an unprecedented concentration of money in the hands of the few.

VI. Financing Structure and Loan Repayment

In a free economy, the prime function of lending by banks is to channel financial resources to the most productive and viable economic uses. To carry out this function successfully credit officers should be capable to assess whether the proposed business plan is likely to be able to repay the loan from operational cash flows. Moreover, bankers will always seek to make any loan as secure as possible. And rightly so, because the funds they lend out are mostly from savers who demand a safe or "risk free" return on their deposits. The price the savers pay for this risk-free return is to be content with receiving a relatively small (but sure) interest rate on their moneys. If they wanted to gamble on attaining higher returns, they could do that but at the greater risk of even losing their investment by taking up equity risk (buy shares in companies).

Many banks however have sought to assess credit risk when considering projects for corporate lending where risk was defined as just the possibility of the lending bank not being able to recover the loan. The accepted practice has been therefore that given a "sound security" position the lender felt comfortable to grant a loan. Repayment capability is a further consideration, but it remains a secondary constraint given that the client can demonstrate that the bank has good available recourse for recovering the loan. This code of conduct has made the banks in Cyprus collateral (or asset backed) lenders rather than business enterprise lenders. The emphasis is firmly on the applicant's balance sheet rather than on the projected income (or cash flow). It is more a question of "show me what you have rather that what you can do". Moreover, credit risk is being assessed by looking at the past (or history) of the applicant rather than the merits and risks of the proposed business plan in the future.

Hence, the expected loss from the operations of a bank should not exceed the bank owners' capital which is the premise on which capital adequacy requirements and the Central Bank's regulatory framework are based on. To put it very simply, banks should not gamble with their depositor clients' moneys. When this happens, then markets crash and world economies, as we have witnessed recently, go into depression spurring a huge reduction and redistribution of wealth.

Because banks need to adhere to the requirement of always being able to return the money received from deposits (plus interest) to the rightful owners, they can only lend money out in a strict and prudent manner. This in effect means that the risk of losing money through a lending operation should be confined only to the limits that can be covered by the capital put up by the bank's owners. Hence, if a bank can reduce the probability of default (through lending only to those who have a capability to repay) and the extent of loss in the event of default (through taking adequate security cover), then they would be able to make more loans and consequently increase the return on the owners' capital. That is the essence of credit risk and its importance of prudent bank lending.

Credit Risk Assessment

Why is it then that banks have relegated repayment capability to a role of secondary importance in credit risk assessment? The simple answer is that it is not easy to assess repayment capability and the risk profile of a project or business. The only way that repayment can be properly assessed is through meaningful cash flow projections. Credit officers should be trained in the methodology and tools of investment appraisal and risk analysis and in addition understand the key success factors and aspects of competitiveness in a business enterprise. The fundamental question is, what would it take for a business venture to be successful in the markets it competes in? This is not a matter of just putting down some numbers on a spreadsheet and calculating what money would remain available for servicing the loans.

A credit officer without the proper training, not just in finance, but also in marketing and management concepts would be at a loss at even asking the right questions let alone judging whether the assumptions made on market projections, prices and market shares are reasonable or not. Moreover, any projection is usually assigned a 100% probability of occurrence. That is by itself an incredible assumption. When contemplating what may occur in the future for anything, not just for businesses forecasts, it is rather naïve to assume that any possible outcome would have but a very minute chance of happening as projected. Even when we are equipped to understand what we are dealing with, at best, we can only assign judgemental probabilities to each possible outcome for each variable in a financial model. But even so, it would be a daunting task to make sense of all scenarios that may arise from the combination all possible outcomes between so many risk variables. Fortunately, by using Monte Carlo simulation software, it is nowadays easy to assess the impact of uncertainty and identify as well as evaluate project risks. Projecting the cash flow within the margins of uncertainty shows how and when it is likely that loan default may arise (as illustrated in Figure 69). This in turn helps the credit officer arrive at an appropriate financing structure for the loan so that it reduces the credit risk and the impact on the Bank in the event of default.

Figure 69 - The Impact of Uncertainty on the Projected Cash flow

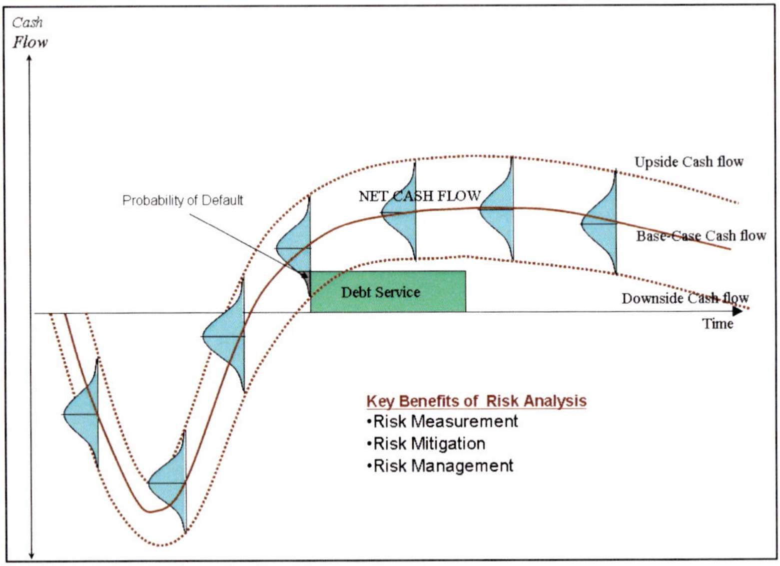

Project Risks

Any business that is seeking finance for a project is subject to several risks. The sources of project risk could be many and varied depending on the project itself and its circumstances such as, the market it will compete in, the type of technology it will use, the financial and economic situation and the legal regime of the countries it will operate in and so on. Project risks can be classified in five categories as indicated in Figure 70.

A proper and thoughtful appraisal of a proposed business plan seen through the prism of a sound financial model that accommodates for risk analysis will reveal and gauge many project risks which can be charted along the projected life of the project and most importantly indicating how they may affect disbursements and loan service during the repayment period (see Figure 71).

Figure 70 - Figure Sources of Project Risk

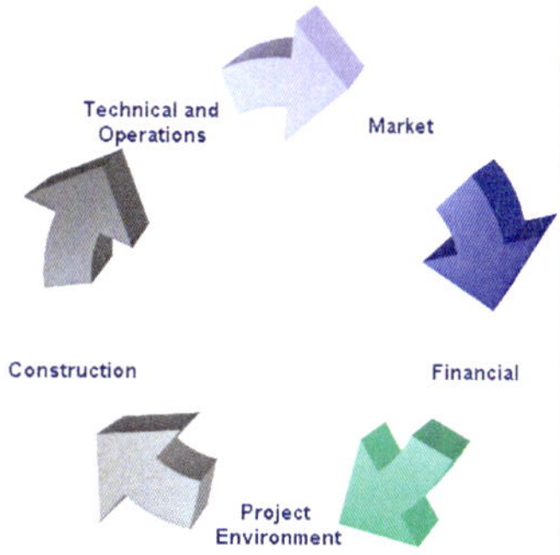

1. **Construction**
   - Cost over-run and delay risk.
   - Experienced and reliable contractor.
   - Availability and cost of building materials.
2. **Technical and Operations**
   - Manageable technology.
   - Availability and cost of supplies, raw materials and energy.
   - Experienced and reliable operator and management personnel.
3. **Market**
   - Existence of a market at the projected quantities and prices.
   - Distribution and transportation of product to market.
   - Adequate communications/promotion channels.
4. **Financial**
   - Currency, foreign exchange risk and inflation.
   - Adequacy of equity contribution.
   - Worth of project assets as a collateral.
5. **Project Environment**
   - Country risk and expropriation risk.
   - Political environment, licences and permits.
   - Force majeure and adequate insurance coverage.

Figure 71 - Project risk phases and financing structure

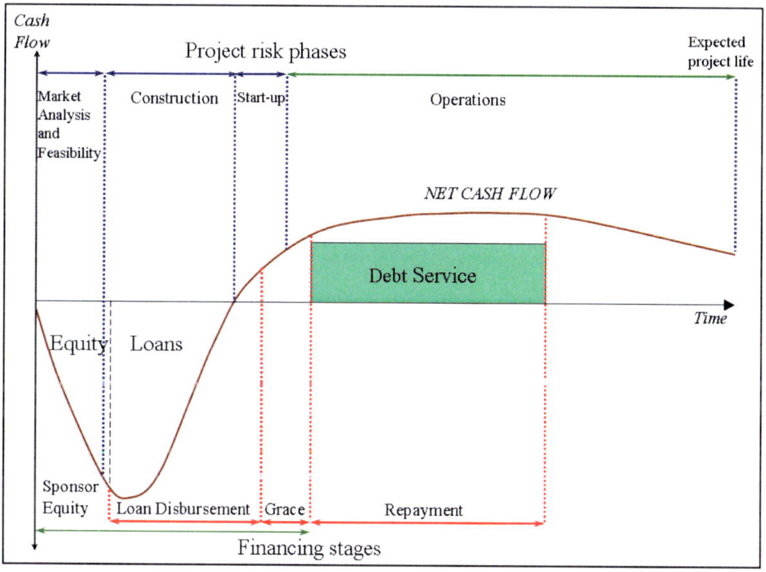

A credit officer can utilise the project risk and financing structure phases framework to identify the risk areas and take appropriate pre-emptive action in the loan contract with the client. There are two distinct stages for which, given that the project risks have been identified and evaluated in the appraisal of the application, the bank can provide for appropriate undertakings and commitments to mitigate and manage credit risk. In the pre-operational stage, full recourse is usually reserved for the lender and in addition several guarantees and undertakings are required to minimise the risks from non-completion and cost over-runs (as illustrated in Figure 72).

Figure 72 - Project risk phases and financing structure - Pre-Operational Stage

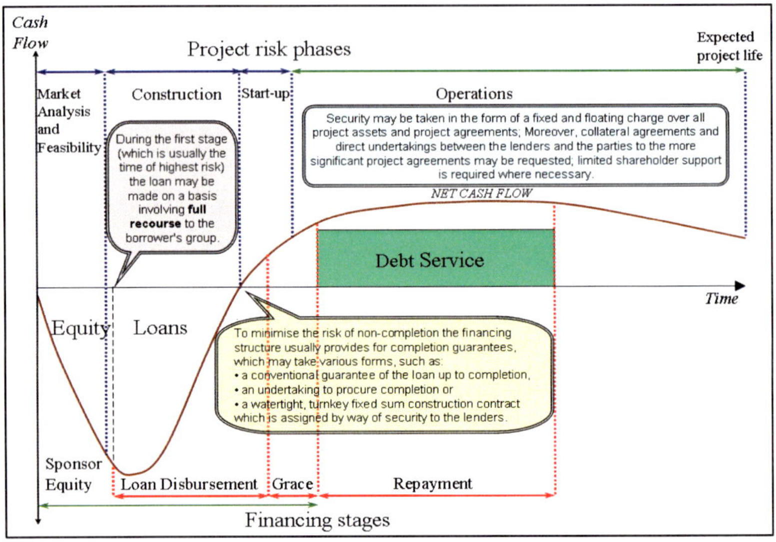

In the operational or post construction stage the bank can reduce the full recourse conditions given that the project meets certain conditions which reduce the risk of non-collection. The full collateral requirements can be further relaxed as the loan is gradually reduced and given that the debt service coverage ratios improve above a pre-agreed level (see Figure 73).

Figure 73 - Project risk phases and financing structure - Operational Stage

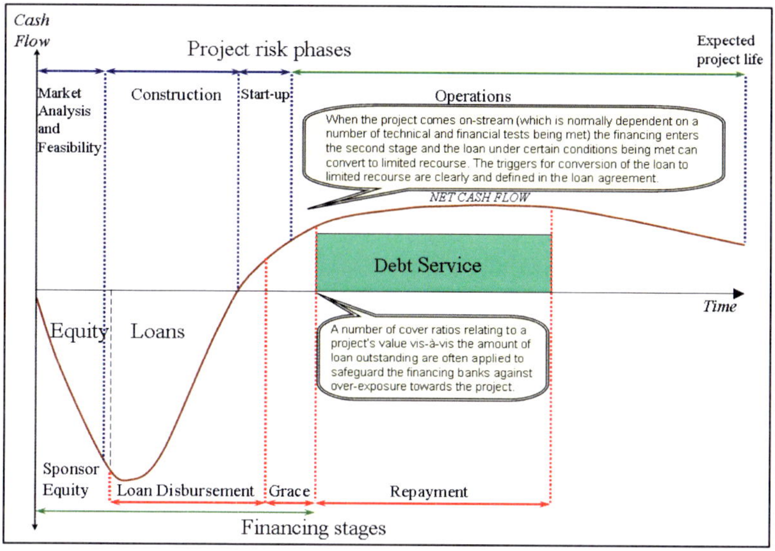

In conclusion, the assessment of credit risk is at the core of corporate lending. It is not a function that can just be delegated to people without the proper training and experience. The long-term success of a bank crucially depends on the quality of work done by its credit officers. Good appraisal and evaluation of the risks during credit risk assessment is likely to have a lasting effect on the quality of the loan portfolio and the ability of the bank to recover in case of default. The only way credit risk can be properly assessed is through cash flow projections which are based on sound financial models and a good understanding of marketing and the aspects of competitiveness in business. Moreover, risk analysis (using the Monte Carlo Simulation methodology) enables the prudent and diligent credit officer to evaluate and map out project risks and take appropriate action in the loan agreement which will ensure that the probability of default is reduced, and the security position of the bank is stronger where it counts most.

VII. The Appraisal of a Capital Investment Project

This chapter is based on the article "The Marketing Evaluation of Capital Investment Projects" published by Savvides, S., in ***World Economics***, Vol. 25, No. 1, January–March 2024

This chapter attempts to put together in one logical and coherent sequence the steps to be followed when attempting to evaluate the competitiveness of an investment project. In summary, the analyst should research and assess the following:

1. What constitutes the **project relevant market** and how it can be defined and measured from both the demand and supply side? A simple formulation is proposed on how to do that in a manner that facilitates the analysis and identifies potential competitors and customers.
2. The determinants of demand and supply reveal the factors that can affect how the market can evolve during the life of the project (or at least for the more immediate years – which are the most crucial in a time-value of money cash flow projection). **Market size and growth** projections can be forecast through assessing the current determinant factors supplementing available statistics and historical price data.
3. The other "ceteris paribus" assumptions such as the homogeneity assumption referring to the product, the constant prices of other products (substitutes and complementary), the constancy of consumer tastes, the instant availability of information and no-cost accessibility to the product, when looked at, through the prism of the **marketing mix** make up (with the addition of the profit margin) the cost and price of the product and are a reflection of an enterprise's final market offering. These are all reflected in cash flow lines in the projections and should be consistent with clear and consistent competitive strategy.
4. The marketing mix and how it relates to the **selection of the appropriate competitive strategy** (product differentiation, cost advantage, or "hybrid") leads to an immediately applicable test of the soundness of the selected competitive strategy for the project as compared to that of its competitors (who have been identified and profiled in *competitor sets* in the relevant market definition, as have consumers in *market segments*).

5. The pillars of a good competitive strategy are:
    a. Developing **market competence** (which really stems from the economic principle of comparative advantage - as it relates to the act of exchange and the economic definition of efficiency in Welfare economics. In other words, the world is better off if people and organisations concentrate in doing what they can be best at and thus develop a competence for adding features to products and services that can generate maximum customer benefits at the lowest possible cost, hence creating customer value and outshifting the project's demand curve.
    b. Optimising **market positioning** by using the elements of the selected marketing mix to effectively target those consumer groups that can best utilise the project market competence and economic situation.
6. Last, but not least, the aim is to create loyal, highly satisfied, customers who become repeat purchasers. To achieve this, the project like a **marketing organisation** must become a self-correcting system having market feedback mechanisms in place and capable of adjusting itself through innovation and strong focus on customer needs to maintain ahead of the competition. Successful projects are invariably those that manage to evolve into marketing organisations.

Introduction

The theory of demand and supply in economics assumes that all products competing in a market are *homogeneous*. Moreover, it also presupposes that consumers have perfect *access* (zero cost in effecting a purchase) as well as perfect *information* (have instant and full knowledge about the product and of any changes in prices in the market). Simply put, this means that all producers and consumers (actual or potential) are presumed to know all there is to know about the market and can therefore take decisions based on the only variables that are allowed to change, which is, Price and Costs of production. Each participant in this highly simplified model of reality is therefore like a poker player who doesn't have to guess the hand of other players, as they all play with open hands and make only logical decisions. Price (and costs), therefore, are the only variables allowed to affect consumer (and supplier) choice in a totally deterministic model of behaviour. This is the only game in town, and it is the driving engine of micro-economic thinking[42].

Market volume and market value are determined where supply meets demand and the market is, by definition, always in equilibrium. Market volume is simply the quantity demanded and supplied (P x Q) at the intersection of the demand and supply curves. Market value (or revenue) is denoted by the area created by Price and Quantity where demand and supply (depicted by down-sloping and up-sloping straight lines respectively) meet (Figure 5).

The product is assumed to be homogeneous, that there are no accessibility costs for consumers (or distribution costs for producers) and that information is totally transparent and instantly available to all concerned in the market. In such a fully deterministic model, the only variable that can change is Price (and costs of production). Quantity demanded and supplied are a function of Price where all the other relevant factors are identified but assumed to remain constant. When considering the costs and benefits from a new project however one cannot assume that these factors are given. The reason is that they form part and are the very substance of the appraisal and often affect the outcome of the project evaluation exercise. Therefore, in addition to Price one should also consider that the products in the market are different, that the sales distribution channel and how the product is perceived are not given and there is a cost associated with these variables that has bearing on the calculation and assumption one makes relating to the projected revenues. Indeed, there are a few possible competitive strategies that a project enterprise can adopt to market its products and services. The important thing to remember is that different marketing strategies in real life may well determine the outcome of the project appraisal (whether in effect a project is deemed to have a positive net worth and an acceptable risk profile).

Just as market conditions are assumed to be given, the demand and supply of a product's market is assumed to be determined by a few economic variables which are again assumed to be constant. The variable that is allowed to change (usually the price of a product) is causing the change in

---

42 The simplified model of reality in economic theory is not presented here as a critique. On the contrary, it is what makes economic thinking a science. Often, it is used to make correct predictions and drive economic decisions and economic policy. In project evaluation, however, it becomes necessary to relax or expand these assumptions into their marketing equivalents (see *Figure 7: Price Theory and the Marketing Mix*) to conduct a proper appraisal for sustainable competitiveness and to analyse the risks facing the project as a business enterprise.

quantity demanded and supplied. Hence, although economic theory recognises that peoples' *tastes*, real *income*, the *price of related goods* and *population* changes can affect market size, it is assumed that they remain constant to facilitate the analysis with respect to the main determinant variable (the price of the product). Similarly, on the supply side, *technology*, *prices of inputs* and *taxes/subsidies* as well as *population* are assumed to be constant (Figure 4).

Some of these assumptions regarding the determinants of demand and supply are relaxed in multi-modal variable demand models which are often constructed and employed by sector experts to forecast expected changes in demand with the introduction of a project, such a toll motorway or a new electricity power plant. These models aim to estimate (quite often by surveying directly the targeted customers opinion) regarding the added value they attach to the incremental benefits that project brings to market. For example, in estimating the additional demand and thereby the "willingness to pay" the higher price for using a new motorway, it is customary to attempt to estimate the added customer value which may result from additional project benefits such as how quickly users of the road reach their destination (value of time), at what operating cost (value of operating cost) and how safely/comfortably they travel (value of safety). From these variables they derive an estimate of the elasticity of demand which they apply to a base case demand growth scenario that is allowed to be determined from such variables such as expected changes in Gross Domestic Product, population in the catchment areas of the project and the increase in car ownership. Alternative modes of transport and competitive reaction to the project is also, at least qualitatively, sought to be taken into consideration.

The result of such models is that there is a base case projection which is allowed to be affected by estimate of the elasticity of demand which is derived through a gallant attempt by industry experts and statisticians to relate and rationalise how a host of variables and the introduction of the new project may affect a "without the project" pattern of demand. Using the elasticity estimate to calculate potential demand is however fraught potential problems.

The term *elasticity* in economics is used to refer to the ratio of the proportional change in one variable with respect to a corresponding proportional change in another variable. Price elasticity of demand is the change in quantity demanded because of a change in price. Economists use this concept to describe and calculate the impact of economic variables on the quantity demanded and supplied in different markets. In project evaluation, the elasticity of demand (and of supply) is used to calculate the weighted average price caused by distortions in the economy that result in a discrepancy between financial and economic prices (or shadow prices).[43] The elasticity of demand is also used to estimate the impact that the release of a new project's supply of products (and services) may have on the market for those products.

In practice, there are a number of difficulties when one tries to apply the concept of elasticity of demand to estimate the impact of a change in a determinant variable:

1. Existing Quantity demanded cannot be used as a base on which to predict a potential change in demand, particularly when a new product or service has not yet had a significant footprint on the existing market. One would have to assume that the elasticity of demand of a revolutionary new product which has the potential to take the market by storm is a near infinite value in order to reflect the possible change in the market from its introduction.[44] To illustrate the point, imagine, for example, if we could turn the clock back and someone came to us with the idea of the Internet or the personal computer as planned new projects and asking us to use such multi-variable demand models to estimate expected demand. I guess the only one who could have predicted that there would be a "pc in every home", and as it turned out, was in position to do something about it, was probably the founder of Microsoft, Bill Gates. Hence, in situations where the impact of a new project is potentially so great that it can redefine, or even create its own market, it is hard to identify which existing markets it even relates to and practically impossible to estimate the magnitude of possible expansion it will spark off. The simple elasticity of demand, both as a concept and as a tool of measurement, therefore, cannot convey the dynamics that can be generated by such innovative projects.
2. A second problem is that a change in Quantity demanded cannot be assumed to be uniform at all points of the demand curve and at various phases of the life cycle of a new product. As a new product goes through a life cycle moving through the introduction, growth and maturity stages of its life the responsiveness of the market to a change in any of the determinant variables of demand changes

---

[43] Harberger, Arnold C., and Glenn P. Jenkins. 2000

[44] Typically, assumed price elasticities of demand vary between -0.5 to -2.

dramatically. As with the example of the personal computer one would probably be correct in estimation a low growth at the time when the Apple computer was introduced but way off the mark after the introduction of the IBM pc (which moved the market from the Introduction to the Growth stage of its development).

3. Finally, while a change in Quantity demanded is not affected by just by a single determinant variable while the others remain constant (all determinant variables affecting the demand of a product act concurrently and impact the Quantity demanded severally and jointly) there is no clear direct relationship of how each variable affects demand and each other so as use to model to demand forecasts. Any model thus derived it is no more than a black box containing several variables that at best interact loosely and vaguely to predict demand.

Decomposing market demand into its constituent parts

There is no accurate definition of a market. This is because all products and services compete to some degree with each other for our limited disposable income. The quest for a proper market definition has therefore proven to be very elusive.[45] The concepts of product substitutability and cross elasticity are used as proxies in defining the boundaries of a market.[46] Depending on the actual need one must satisfy one may be willing to exchange anything to get it.[47] So therefore even "substitutability" is not a good factor for defining a market. Yet, even in the rare occasions where the data are available to facilitate such analysis it is still not at all clear what delineates one market from another. National and other statistics usually account and classify industries by a loose definition based on the physical characteristics of products. For the purposes of project evaluation and Business planning in general this however is hardly a sufficient base on which to project revenues and costs.

[45] Fischer. 1997

[46] Smits. 1958

[47] This is exemplified in the exclamation from the play *King Richard III*, by William Shakespeare where the king cries out, "A horse! A horse! My kingdom for a horse!" after his horse is killed in battle, leaving him at the mercy of his enemies.

Figure 74 - The Market Size Analysed by Market Segment

Market Penetration X Usage X Price = Market Value

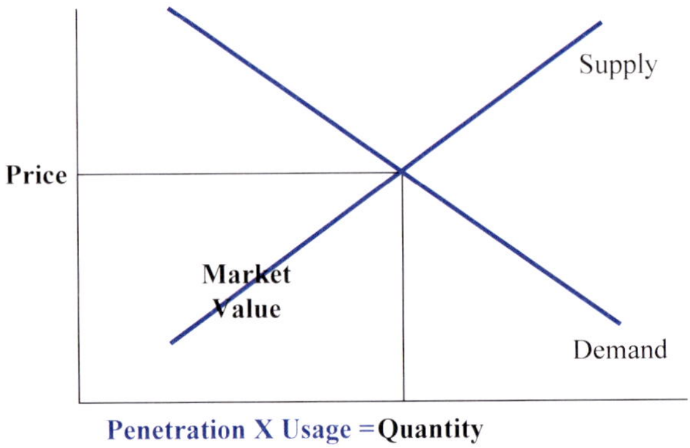

In addition to the *ceteris paribus* assumptions, micro-economic analysis uses an aggregate or composite variable in the term *Quantity* demanded. However, quantity demanded is really the product of two market variables –the *number of customers* (or users) of the product times the *take-up rate* or level of purchases during the period considered. Let's call the former *market penetration* and the latter *Usage*. Market analysis in this fashion is facilitated through the break-down of the market in market segments (or basically homogeneous clusters of customers – actual or potential) that are characterized by similar and predictable market behaviour. It is necessary to disaggregate the data to the level of component market segments, market penetration and usage to apply pertinent marketing and competitive analysis to one's projections. Moreover, this is often the only way to identify the relevant risk variables and facilitate the application of Monte Carlo simulation risk analysis[48] to assess, mitigate and manage market risk in new capital investment projects.

Although it is possible to use this type of analysis on the total population (where the take-up rate or usage of non-customers may be taken as zero) it is practical and useful to reduce the population to the level of the potential and relevant market for the project[49]. The difference between the former and

---

[48] Savvakis C. Savvides. 1994

[49] Savvakis C. Savvides. 2000

the latter is that part of the population which may reasonably be outside of the scope and influence of the marketing mix (price, product, distribution and communications policies) of the project and its main competitors' activities. It should also be pointed out that in the case of completely new and innovative products it may well be that actual market penetration (at least for some of the market segments comprising the total relevant market) is very low or practically non-existent. Indeed, this is why it is imperative to apply this type of analysis to understand the market drivers and truly calculate the potential revenues for the project's products and services.

The market analysis for a new project should therefore be applied in a framework where:

- Main market segments are identified and clearly defined.
- Market penetration and usage are estimated through desk research and simple fieldwork if necessary.
- Prices (including the project's position on the other marketing mix elements or variables[50]) for each market segment and product are decided as part of the project's Business plan.

Thus, quantity demanded is analysed and estimated based on *Usage* and *Market Penetration* with respect to each of the component market segments making up the total relevant market. Quantity demanded is the product of these two variables (and is shown as the two-dimensional rectangle at the bottom of the box in the diagram depicted in Figure 75). When multiplied by the third variable *Price* this gives the total Market Value (or Revenue) for that market segment.

Projected market revenues for the total relevant market are therefore the sum of the products of Market Penetration, Usage and Price of each component market segment, as illustrated in Figure 76.

What is the significance of disaggregating the data to the level of Usage and Market penetration? It is not simply because these two marketing variables can easily be estimated through a combination of available secondary data supplemented by simple fieldwork. Almost equally important is the fact that to use this methodology one needs to go through the steps and discipline of understanding how the market works. One first needs to identify basically homogeneous clusters of customer groups and build the market potential

[50] A pertinent strategic analysis can only take place with the project being disaggregated and analysed down to its main marketing components.

from bottom up. This framework lays the foundations for strategic marketing analysis in project evaluation. It forces the analyst to ask the right questions and to come up with answers that can potentially reveal the driving forces and key competences that can make a project successful in its environment.

Figure 75 - Price and Quantity where (Q = Usage x Market Penetration)

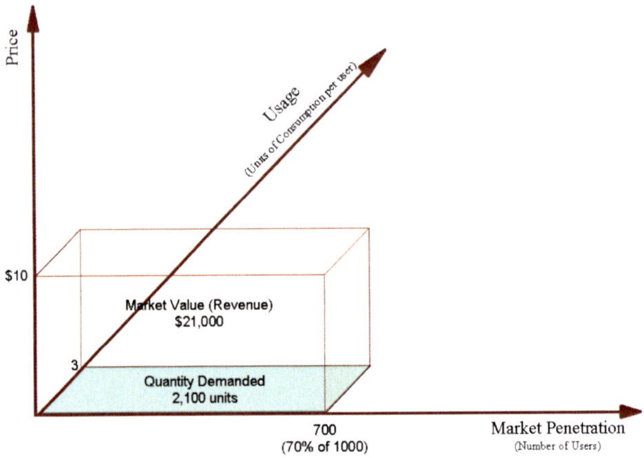

Figure 76 - Bottom-up Calculation of Quantity Demanded

Market Segment	Market Penetration		Usage or Take Up Rate		Quantity Demanded		Price		Market Revenue
MS1		X		=	Q1	X	P1	=	MR1
MS2		X		=	Q2	X	P2	=	MR2
MS3		X		=	Q3	X	P3	=	MR3
Market Size					Total Volume				Total Value

Market size - Demand

$$Md = \sum_{i=1}^{n} (D_i)(Q_i)(P_i)$$

Market size - Supply

Where:

$$Ms = \sum_{i=1}^{n} (S_i)(Q_i)(P_i)$$

$D = Demanders$

$S = Suppliers$

$Q = Quantity$

$P = Price$

The relationship between Marketing and Economics

Marketing relaxes the *ceteris paribus* assumptions of Price Theory. As a result, some of the clarity of analysis that is attained by assuming several unrealistic, yet key assumptions as given is lost and replaced by a model that resembles reality more closely but which nevertheless, like reality, is uncertain and not always yielding correct predictions. We thus move from the deterministic comfort of micro-economic theory to the "risky" or probabilistic world of Marketing and Organisational competitiveness. Yet, this trade-off is necessary when one must deal with the strategic decisions that present themselves in the context of business strategy and therefore in project evaluation. Moreover, in the application of investment appraisal, the two disciplines (Price theory and Marketing) are not, in the opinion of the author mutually exclusive. Marketing was weaved out of the easing of the ceteris paribus assumptions of price theory.

To identify the underlying marketing forces and assess project competitiveness and risk one must consider the issues that emerge from relaxing the assumptions of micro-economic theory. There is no perfect information Firms incur costs to develop and pass their messages to their targeted customers. The Promotion mix of each competitor imposes different costs and has varying effectiveness on the market. Similarly, the distribution channels companies put in place add costs and create different benefits to users of the product accordingly. Even pricing becomes a tool in the hands of competitors in the market to attract consumers to their products while achieving their profit objectives. Finally, there are no homogeneous products. Every product is different, and firms do their utmost to differentiate their products by building in features that seem to give what their targeted market wants to have. Even commodities are or are perceived to be differentiated. And what consumer perception is what really matters as far as consumer choice is concerned. Hence, with a proper strategic assessment of the project's marketing mix elements as compared to those of its typical competitors (as shown in Figure 19) a firm can position itself in the market to optimise its potential.

The challenge is to replace the rather restrictive Price theory assumptions with their corresponding Marketing Mix counterparts while maintaining the clarity of analysis and useful directions that Economic theory can provide. It will be shown that it is indeed possible, when you analyse the relevant market by segment to do this by enriching the model for each market segment with the possible impact that each marketing mix element can have on both the Supply and Demand of the project. The analysis would be no different than the one an economist uses to calculate the impact of subsidies, taxes and other economic distortions have on the price (and quantity) of a market. It should thus integrate well with the economic analysis as theorised and applied in project evaluation.

The marketing mix elements can affect the demand and supply function of a project's market in a predictable way. Resources used to add features to the product or services of the project have the effect of shifting the Supply and Demand curves of the project in opposite directions (as illustrated in Figure 61). If successful, the measures causing these added costs which push the Supply curve inwards manage also to shift the Demand curve outwards to cause a net benefit. Adding more quality (or functionality) to the product and/or expanding the available distribution channels to reach more customers and/or funding a new advertising and promotional campaign that aims to inform and persuade the targeted group of potential customers to buy the product all independently and collectively manifest themselves in the projected cash flows as additional capital and operational expenditure. An increase in revenues results from a higher quantity demanded and quite possibly the higher Price that users now are willing to pay (as illustrated in Figure 61). The increase in quantity demanded results either through increased Usage (higher consumption per person) and/or Market Penetration (by attracting new customers).

A quick cost benefit analysis on an incremental set of measures should always be done prior to the adoption of increase in scale or change of the project design (either in the capital or operational expenditure part). To the extent that a project succeeds in creating net benefits it also causes a market expansion.

Figure 77 - Adding Marketing Mix Features affects both Demand and Supply

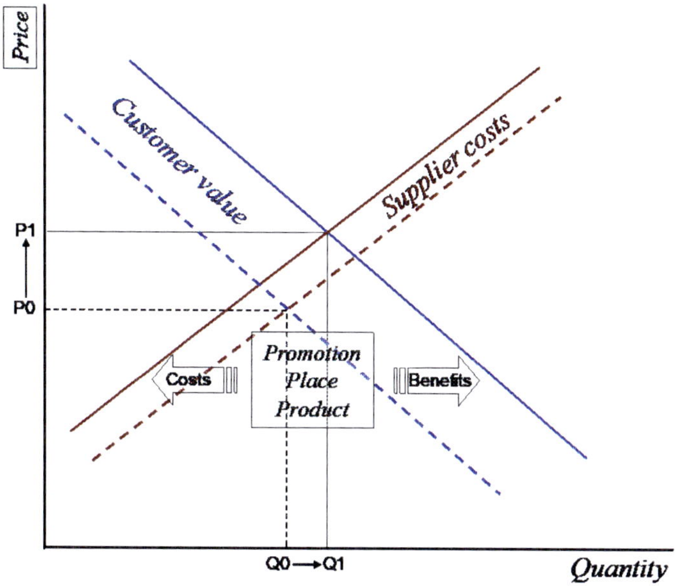

Market Profiling: Market segments and Competitor sets

The foundations of the proposed methodology lay in the "typification" of the market players on both the demand and supply side of the market as it relates to the project. This involves a market profiling exercise that leads towards the identification and measurement of relevant to the project *market segments* and *competitor sets*. Market segments should be arrived at having as guide the fundamental market need that project aims to satisfy.[51] The choice of market segmentation to be used is in practice largely determined by the availability of data and the ease with which pertinent market statistics can be gathered.

[51] Savvakis C. Savvides. 1990

Figure 78 - Determining total market demand and supply

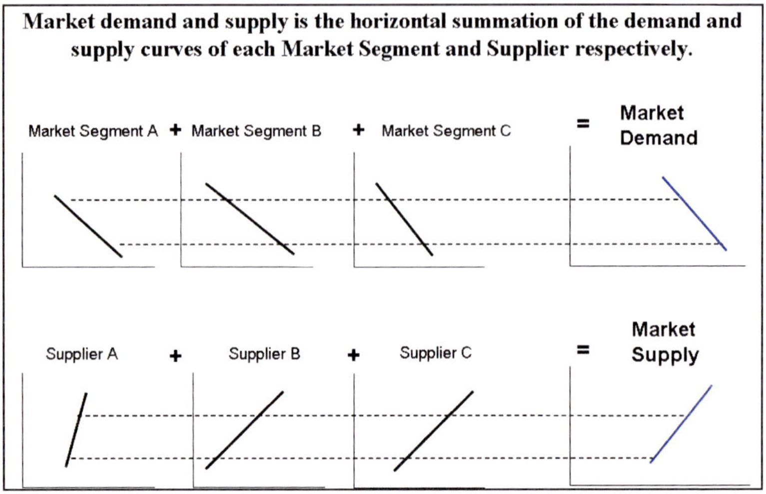

Figure 79 - Determining market demand and supply with project

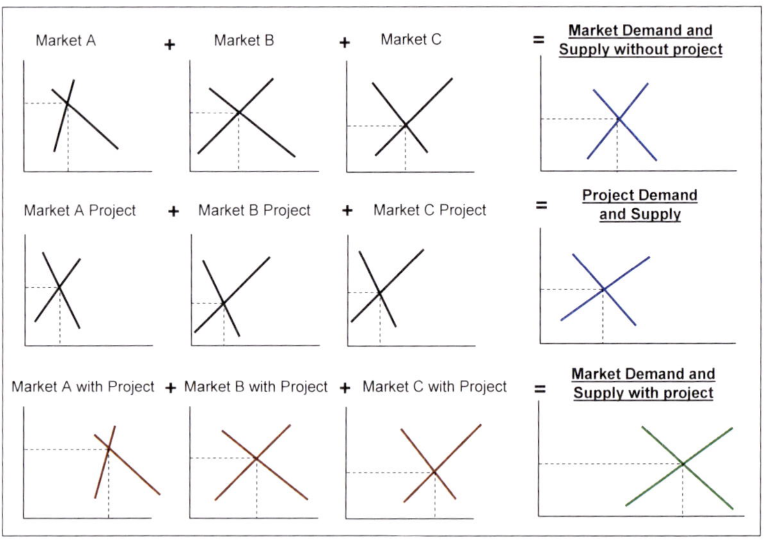

Marketing performance and strategic appraisal

The above analysis, if properly done, will lead to questions that can be considered and facilitated by a Marketing Performance Box (Figure 80).

Figure 80 - The Marketing Performance Box

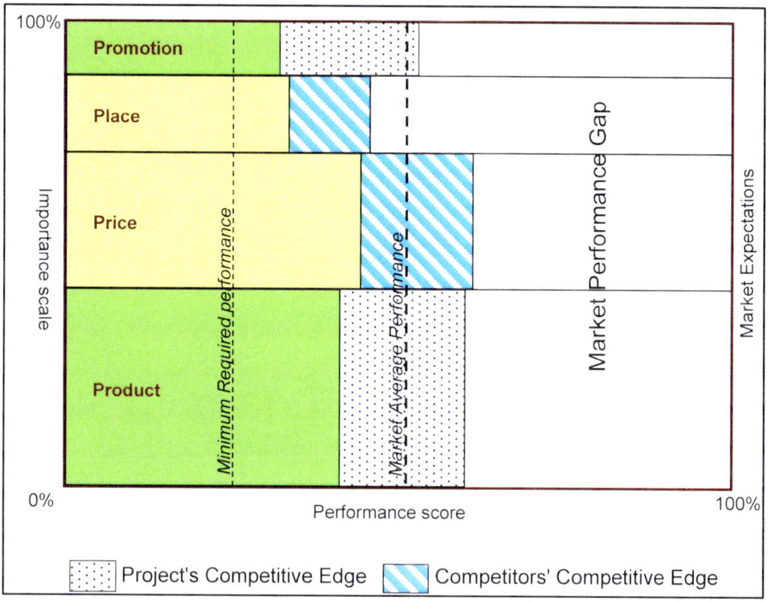

The Marketing Organisation

The essence of marketing analysis can only find an expression and its potential be realised in the market through what we call a Marketing Organisation. By this we mean that sustainable competitiveness can only be attained if the organisation undertaking the project is marketing oriented and builds systems which can ensure that market needs and competitive activity are properly tracked and the capability of the organisation to respond to new marketing challenges arising from the emergence of market performance gaps are enhanced and maintained. To do this effectively, the organisation should perceive itself as an organic system responding to changes in its market environment. Figure 81 shows the full cycle that the learning marketing organisation should adopt and define its existence in the market.

Figure 81 - The Marketing Organisation

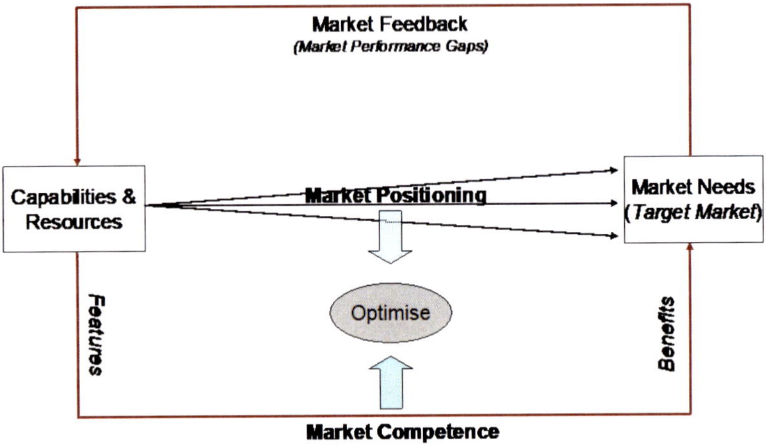

Marketing analysis as applied in investment appraisal

We will now try to demonstrate the impact of marketing analysis in project appraisal through an example:

A recurring theme in tutorial workshops lead by the author recently[52], where four different case studies in investment appraisal were examined, was the need for this type of market analysis in project evaluation to estimate project revenues and facilitate a proper assessment of project market risk. Indeed, the example used to demonstrate the application of the proposed methodology was inspired by one of these case studies which involved the building of a toll road in Uruguay that would link the capital of Argentina Buenos Aires and Sao Paulo the largest port in Brazil and significantly shorten the road distance and travel time between the two cities.[53] Only the actual market segmentation and proposed toll structure as at the year 1999 have been maintained as reported in (*Alberto Barreix, Glenn P. Jenkins, and Mario Marchesini 2003).*

As this is simply a demonstration of how the methodology should be applied, the number of potential users, take up rates and market penetration

---

[52] Where the author was a visiting lecturer on the Program in Investment Appraisal and Risk Analysis held in June–July 2007 at the John Deutch Centre, Queens University, Kingston, Ontario.

[53] *Alberto Barreix, Glenn P. Jenkins, and Mario Marchesini 2003*

levels assumed in the example are arbitrary and used only to demonstrate the application of the methodology. This was necessary, as there were no data available regarding the potential market users or level of usage on which to base a more realistic estimate for the market penetration levels. The case study, as it is often the case with many project appraisal efforts, attempted to estimate the Quantity demanded directly by sizing up the number of vehicle kilometres or the number of trips expected for each market segment. No direct or implied reference was made to the two key variables of *market penetration* and *usage* that are core variables in the proposed methodology. The numbers used in this example therefore have no relevance to the real situation in these three countries which still needs to be researched if it is to be properly applied to the situation of the current project.

The units of analysis were taken to be the five sections of the road for which the Uruguayan Government decided to charge toll fares for. Each section and type of vehicle combination is therefore like a different product in the full product line offered by the new project. Thus, a track going the full distance between Buenos Aires and Sao Paulo would buy five product units and pay five tolls as priced for that vehicle[54]. Table 6 shows the price structure for each market segment (type of vehicle) with respect to each of the five sections of the road[55].

The analysis should estimate the market with and without the project. The difference between the two should give us the incremental project revenues (and volumes) resulting from the project. This is illustrated in Tables 5 to 6. It should be noted that in this example, Usage is assumed to increase more substantially for heavy tracks before and after the project as it maybe anticipated that an increase in the demand for cargo between Argentina and Brazil would mean that each track will have to go the full distance (all five sections of the new road).

The number of tracks comprising the potential market were assumed to be only a mere 50,000 and 30,000 respectively for light and heavy tracks. Nevertheless, market penetration in the freight market was assumed in this example to increase to the same high level as that of the passenger segments

[54] The average price for each type of vehicle was assumed for simplicity.

[55] Using this example, it would be possible for the project team to gather the correct data from the source countries and through simple fieldwork survey the usage levels for each market segment. The pricing was also assumed to be different according to the type of vehicle and length of trip. The pricing of the project services is a decision variable impacting the optimisation of the potential revenues and costs of the project.

(i.e., 70% of potential market). This may be justified if the new road and bridge combination are indeed capable of creating efficient economic conditions for export trade between the three countries (but between the two large countries of Argentina and Brazil). The usage rates would be expected to change following the implementation of a project to the extent that the new products and services add significant novelty and customer value that encourages customers to increase their usage or consumption levels. This assumption, as well as the level of market penetration should be investigated through asking directly a sample of potential users from each market segment questions regarding the frequency, length of use as well as their willingness to pay at various prices before and after the project.

Table 5 - Toll Structure for a Highway Project

Table 3.7. Proposed Toll Structure
(1999 Ur$)

Project section	Cars	Buses	Trucks (2 or 3 axles)	Trucks (4 or more axles)
1	64	111	143	210
2	46	74	95	115
3	42	63	87	110
4	39	62	73	91
5	59	88	170	217
Total	*250*	*398*	*217*	*743*

Note: The proposed toll structure includes value added tax.
Source: BCEOM (1998).

Table 6 - Market Performance without Project

Market Segment	Potential Market	Market Penetration		Usage or Take Up Rate		Quantity Demanded		Price *		Market Revenue
Passenger Cars	1,000,000	60%	X	3	=	1,800,000	X	25	=	45,000,000
Buses	15,000	50%	X	10	=	75,000	X	40	=	2,985,000
Light Tracks	50,000	25%	X	20	=	250,000	X	22	=	5,425,000
Heavy Tracks	30,000	15%	X	30	=	135,000	X	74	=	10,030,500
Market Size						2,260,000				63,440,500

* *Is is assumed that toll fares would be 50% without the project*

Table 7 - Market Performance with Project

Market Segment	Potential Market	Market Penetration		Usage or Take Up Rate		Quantity Demanded		Price		Market Revenue
Passenger Cars	1,000,000	70%	X	5	=	3,500,000	X	50	=	175,000,000
Buses	15,000	70%	X	15	=	157,500	X	80	=	12,537,000
Light Tracks	50,000	70%	X	30	=	1,050,000	X	43	=	45,570,000
Heavy Tracks	30,000	70%	X	50	=	1,050,000	X	149	=	156,030,000
Market Size						5,757,500				389,137,000

Table 8 - Incremental Market Development due to Project

Market Segment	Potential Market	Market Penetration		Usage or Take Up Rate		Quantity Demanded		Price		Market Revenue
Passenger Cars	1,000,000	10%	X	2	=	1,700,000	X	25	=	130,000,000
Buses	15,000	20%	X	5	=	82,500	X	40	=	9,552,000
Light Tracks	50,000	45%	X	10	=	800,000	X	22	=	40,145,000
Heavy Tracks	30,000	55%	X	20	=	915,000	X	74	=	145,999,500
Market Size						3,497,500				325,696,500

It should be noted that after allowing the market penetration of each segment and the usage to increase at a future time after completion of the project, the incremental revenues of each customer group are shown to change significantly. Because of the assumed prior to the project low market penetration of tracks (particularly heavy tracks) the potential for the project to generate revenues and expand the market is likely to come from the business rather than the passenger traffic. Moreover, the elasticity of demand in cases, such as this, where the existing market penetration is very low, is very unlikely to reproduce what may be possible to be attained. The reason is because the elasticity of demand is calculated as a proportion on the existing quantities and market magnitudes. This paradox is highlighted in extreme cases where the potential of market adoption of a product which is completely new, can hardly be reflected using elasticity of demand as the existing quantity demanded is very small (as in the case of heavy tracks in the example) or practically zero. Even though elasticity can vary from 0 to infinity, it would be hard, if not absolutely impossible, to guesstimate what the elasticity should be without first analysing the market to its basic component market segments (in terms of market penetration and usage).[56]

The procedure one should follow to gather the data for the key market variables in the example used here would be the following:

1. Gather hard data on the number of vehicles by each category used in the example for Argentina, Uruguay and Brazil (and possibly Chile). Information regarding the owners of these vehicles (whether households or businesses) should also be collected.[57] Analysis by type of business and possibly geographical location for each of these countries should be available through publicly available national industrial and population statistics. The latter should be used to trim down the total numbers to the relevant to the project potential market for each market segment by including only those geographical locations and types of businesses that can reasonably be expected to be using the new road.[58] The total population figures including the proportion of these that is taken to be the potential market for each market segment should be reported.
2. Estimate the level of current market penetration for each market segment by seeking available traffic statistics. If these data are not available, the information may be gathered through adding relevant questions in the survey questionnaire which should also ask how usage may change at the proposed (or considered) prices for the project.
3. The usage data maybe collected by constructing semantic scales ranging from "Never" to what may be considered a maximum usage (for instance: "100 sections or more" for a year). Once enough data are gathered in this manner a frequency distribution for Usage will begin to emerge for each category. This can also be used as the

---

[56] Savvakis C. Savvides. 1990

[57] In the case of Buses (which may be for commuting or leisure purposes) potential organisers such as tour operators maybe outside the geographical area of the countries concerned. The new road and bridge may become the base on which international tour operators may develop high customer value tourist packages.

[58] It should be noted that even if the totals of the market are used as proxies to the potential market (before first reducing the numbers down to what may be directly relevant to the project) the analysis still holds. It would simply mean that market penetration assumptions would not be expected to be reaching anywhere near the maximum 100% and that the usage rate would be significantly smaller because a representative sample of the overall population would now include many respondents with very low take up rates.

probability distribution in the risk analysis if Usage is a risk variable.

4. Market penetration levels should increase during the first years of the project possibly following an S shape path. The more innovative or novel the product of the project the more likely it will follow an S shape path (where initially, going through an introduction period only a small of adopters can be expected following which a Growth period of rapid acceleration would follow). In the case of the motorway in Uruguay and bridge combination linking it to Argentina, the service offered are not considered to be in essence any different from those that are offered by other routes or shipping modes in the case of cargo. The real benefit would result from the economies to be derived from savings and convenience in transportation vis-à-vis existing alternative methods.

It should also be possible to aggregate back to the market demand curve by adding horizontally (as shown in Figure 62) the constituent market segments. The elasticity of demand for the combined market demand curve would then be reflected in the shape of the new aggregate demand curve. Similarly, the competitive analysis profiles of the suppliers can also be analysed and aggregated back to the industry of market supply curve in the same fashion.

The benefits of the marketing approach to project evaluation

Decomposing the market demand curve into its constituent parts (by market segment and in terms of market penetration and usage) allows the analysis to identify market drivers and measure the real potential demand and the willingness to pay at various prices. It inevitably means that some market research is necessary to establish the component market variables for each market segment. But since this would be focused market research, aiming to establish the actual numbers belonging to an identified group (market penetration) and the usage, or potential consumption, of a product or service it should not be too difficult to structure and execute. Even a very simple questionnaire administered on a small sample from each market segment can yield a much better estimate of demand than trying to guess directly the aggregate quantity demanded from published statistics or to use an elasticity that disregards the question of how many are or could be members of a customer group and what would be their potential usage at different prices.

Having extracted an estimate for the three component market determinants of Market Penetration, Usage and Price it should be possible to sketch the shape of demand curve for each market segment. These can be used directly in the financial model estimating the cash flow projections or even by aggregating to the market demand curve through adding them up. The elasticity of demand used in the economic analysis would thus be derived directly from the market analysis relating directly to the project at hand rather than from general historical or other market data available.

Finally, such an analysis should identify the important market parameters that can be used as risk variables to apply sensible and coherent sensitivity and risk analysis to the base case model. Market risk would thus be better assessed and possibly mitigated if it is possible to deal directly with market penetration, usage and price rather than assuming an elasticity of demand and trying to guess how quantity demanded itself would vary. In the final analysis, no matter how good the methodology applied, a better project evaluation can only take place if we develop the skills to understand how the market is made up and the factors that drive it.

There are many sophisticated techniques and scientific models one can employ to analyse and forecast demand.[59] They do not however guarantee a better prediction and very often are overkill to a situation where logic and simple fieldwork should prevail and, in the author's experience, be preferred. There is no substitute to market related common sense. We can do a lot to improve the accuracy and relevance of our projections. What is proposed in this paper is simple, relevant and always applicable. All markets can be analysed in this manner. It should be a lot easier to venture a projection from an estimated pool of potential customers and their buying habits than it is to try to estimate how quantity will change without regard to these basic components of market revenue. Indeed, setting a project evaluation study in such a framework facilitates strategic and competitive analysis. This in turn creates the conditions for a more thoughtful approach to the problem. When the unit of analysis is the customer, actual and potential, and the question is asked whether and under which conditions it is possible to switch to the products of the project, then it is inevitable to also ask how competitors will react and why the project would be able to survive in such conditions.[60] It is also easier to estimate the level of market

---

[59] See for example, *Zhineng Hu. 2006 or Namwoon Kim, Rajendra K. Srivastava, Jin K. Han. 1999*

[60] Something which apparently the Eurotunnel studies did not ask or really provided adequate answers for.

expansion that the project is likely to generate.

Conclusion

The analysis aimed to show that there is a real need to disaggregate a project's market into its basic components to identify and measure the impact it is likely to have on the existing market and to facilitate the cash flow projections (both revenues and costs).

The need to analyse and research the market cannot be over emphasised in cases where a project is to introduce a significant innovation or novelty in the market. The theory of diffusion of innovations is generally accepted and well documented in marketing literature.[61] The introduction of new products and services is likely to have a significant impact not only on the revenues of the project but also, assuming a coherent marketing and competitive strategic plan, on the costs or cash outflows part of the projections. The marketing mix strategies for introducing new products invariably mean that an appropriate expenditure budget should be in place to support the introduction of a new product or service at the various phases of its projected life cycle.

[61] *Everett Rogers. 2003*

VIII. Risk Analysis and Project Financing

Any new project's outcome is uncertain. It is therefore desirable to evaluate the impact of alternative possible scenarios considering the risks that are intrinsic to the project and ask whether there is the capability to overcome them and therefore attain and sustain a competitive advantage. In other words, any new investment project should have a manageable risk profile and the decision whether to undertake (and finance it) should depend on the outcome of this appraisal and risk analysis[62]. If the project risks are properly identified and measured it is often possible to seek and find suitable solutions to mitigate and manage it among the different stakeholders of the project. Figure 82 outlines the typical risks that a project is subject to, and which must be assessed before the capital investment and finance decision is taken[63]:

Figure 82 - Sources of Project Risk

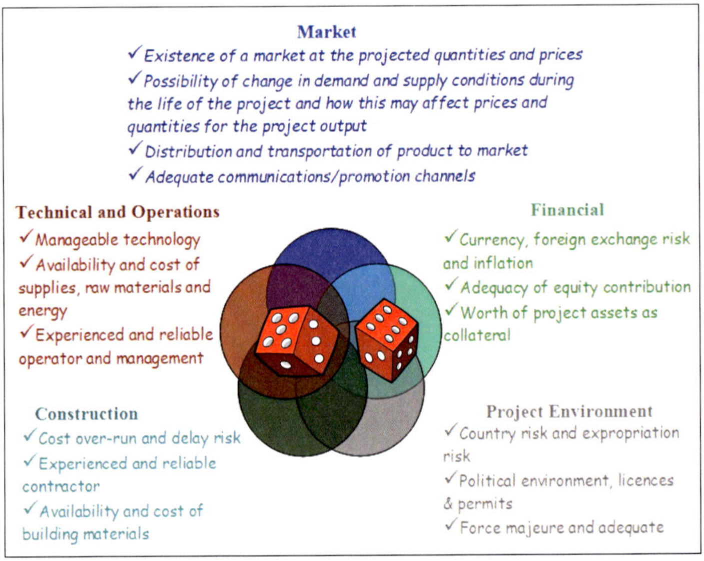

[62] For the methodology of Risk Analysis in Investment Appraisal see Savvides, S C. 1994

[63] For an exposition on Analysing and providing for Market Risk in Project Evaluation see Savvides, S C. 2000

A proper and thoughtful appraisal of a proposed business plan seen through the prism of a sound financial model that accommodates for risk analysis will reveal and gauge a number of inherent risks which can be charted along the projected life of the project and most importantly from the point of view of the lending bank indicate how these may affect loan disbursements and loan service during the repayment period[64] (see Figure 83)[65].

Figure 83 - Risk Analysis on Projected Cash Flow

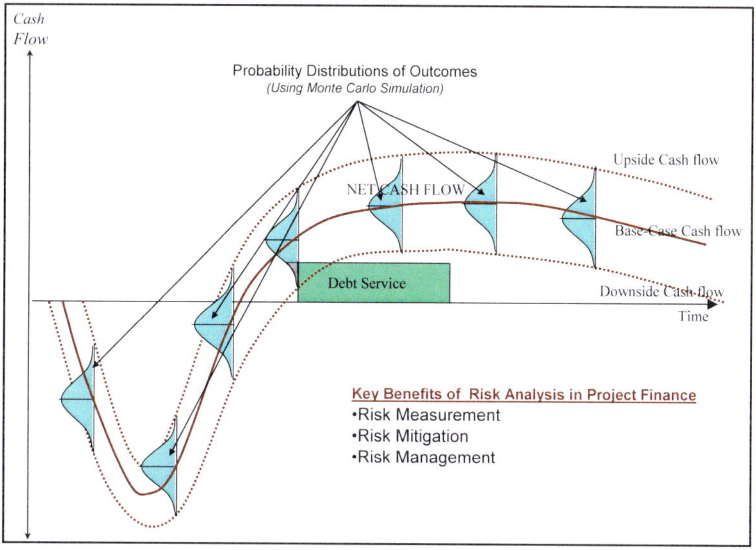

Sustainable economic development therefore can only be attained if capital investment and financing is directed towards funding the most viable and ergo competitive projects. Real economic development comes from building on solid grounds and from funding projects which add net customer value and are cost effective. Only viable and competitive projects promote the cause of economic development. This holds true for both foreign and local investment projects. An investment in a project which is likely to foreclose before its expected life span or that is likely to be unable to repay its loans only drags the economy even further into recession.

[64] For complete case-studies that include financial, economic and risk analysis see: Andreas Andreou, Glenn Jenkins, Savvakis C. Savvides and 1990 and Andreas Andreou, Glenn Jenkins, Savvakis C. Savvides. 1991.

[65] Source: Savvides, S C. 2011

Project Stakeholders Analysis

The cash flow projections of any investment project should be looked at with respect to its different project stakeholders[66]. The "Owner" of the project which includes the loans and other inflows and outflows relating to the owners of the project, the "Banker" (or Total Investment view) where it is assumed that the project is all equity funded in order to show how good the project may be in supporting the repayment of its obligations (including the loans it may wish to raise). And finally, the "Economy's View" where the basic cash flow is adapted and the prices adjusted to reflect the net benefits and costs arising to the Economy in general. Economic value (which is the building block of economic development) occurs when the net present value arising from the costs and benefits cash flow of a project from the Economy's perspective is positive.

Economic development therefore stems from investing and funding economically viable projects. It does not come about because a foreign or local investor is persuaded, or "bribed", to invest in a project he would never have invested in without the special concessions, subsidies, relaxations and tax exemptions that may have been made by an uninformed and over-eager government to attract foreign investment. This happens time and again where a public sector Concession Authority does not understand the distinction between an economically viable vis-à-vis a financially plausible from the Owner's point of view investment project. But bureaucrats and politicians, conveniently for them, still fail to understand that non-viable investment projects inevitably only drag the economy even further into recession.

The requirement to identify, appraise and finance developmentally strong projects is even greater when there is a crying need for restructuring to get the economy out of recession. In such circumstances, a government should be ready to make the necessary reforms and put in place those mechanisms necessary to facilitate this critical process for spearheading economic development. These may include the better regulation of banks to focus on their core savings and lending activities and the retraining/reorganisation necessary to enhance their capability to assess credit risk for restructuring existing loans and for granting new ones (Savvides 2011). It may also consider the creation of a Reconstruction and Development Bank to take steps to secure and position long term funds and lead the way in the financing of major projects in the economy in a new development initiative.

---

[66] Jenkins, G.P., 1998. and Glenday, G., 1998

Finally, the Government should create its own capability to have independent expert advice on the structuring, evaluation and financing of public sector and Public-Private-Partnership (PPP) projects and for managing the project development and procurement process. Without a competent and totally independent professional body (such as a National Advisory and Finance Agency) it is practically impossible to ensure that the public is receiving value for money from a privatisation or a PPP project. Indeed, a newly created Development Bank in the model of the German KFW Bank can serve both as a lender to industry and as advisor to the Government on Public Sector and PPP projects. In the final analysis the Government should understand that economic development is best served when capital investment, whether from the Public or Private sector, is directed towards projects which are economically viable for the country under free market competitive conditions.

Evaluating and pricing contracts in project finance

The norm for contracts and guarantees among various stakeholder in a capital investment project is that the parties should reach an agreement whereby those who can better manage some of the project risks would be the ones to undertake them. But there is a price attached to all such agreements. This is particularly evident in projects between private investors and a Public sector entity or more commonly referred to as Public-Private-Partnerships (PPPs).

The purpose of this chapter is twofold. The first is to demonstrate how a well-designed Monte Carlo simulation software such as *RiskEase©* by RiskEase Ltd (see Appendix) can be used in a manner to enhance and facilitate decision making in project finance deals among various stakeholders. This is particularly needed in cases between a Public sector entity and a private enterprise in a Public-Private-Partnership deal (PPPs). But the most important purpose for working through a real example of a mega real-life project finance capital investment is to demonstrate how the application of the methodology of Monte Carlo simulation is used prudently to go beyond the constraints of single value appraisals and thereby to explore and consider mutually beneficial contracts between the project parties[67].

[67] The example has been constructed from a real motorway project in Greece in 2008. *Some projections have of course been amended to comply with confidentiality commitments. But not to the extent as to change or conceal the real issues at play or*

Evaluation of Guarantee in a Public-Private Project

As an example of how Monte Carlo simulation can be used to assess risk and price contracts a real motorway project case is presented below. An outline of the key steps and the main points raised are highlighted with explanations where necessary. It also demonstrates a way through which to evaluate and price a contract in project finance.

The proposed contract was aimed in putting in place a guarantee from the Government to the company that was to undertake the motorway project to make the return and risk acceptable to the project owner (and enable the project to be implemented). It is presumed that, for the purposes of this case, the motorway was found to have a positive Economic Net Present Value. The Government provided a guarantee for a minimum number of trips to the Project Owner for each of four types of vehicles. The Integrated Financial Model© by RiskEase Ltd was used to model the projections and **RiskEase**© *Master Edition* software to apply the risk analysis. The project assumed that a government guarantee will be in place to cover a large part of the downside risk for the Project Owner.

The Financial Model was set up to calculate with a switch the results for the main stakeholders (Owner and Economy) without the guarantee (**wo**) and with the guarantee (**wg**) in place. In the latter set it was assumed that any scenarios generated during the simulation that were below the minimum agreed level of traffic that the government would guarantee the Owner of the project will be compensated accordingly. The two simulations (without and with the guarantee in place) would then be combined and compared as illustrated in Figure 84.

The methodology for valuing guarantees or other contractual agreements in project finance is through setting up, running and comparing two simulations. One without the agreement and one where the impact of such an undertaking is modelled into the projections. The present value and the risk profile of the project in the two simulations is then calculated and compared. The value of the contract is the difference in the two expected NPVs.

---

the lessons learnt from studying this project. My involvement as Head of the Project Financing Division of the Cyprus Development Bank at the time was in assessing it from the point of view of a financier who was invited to be a participant in a syndicated loan for this project.

Figure 84 - Modelling the simulation without and with a Guarantee

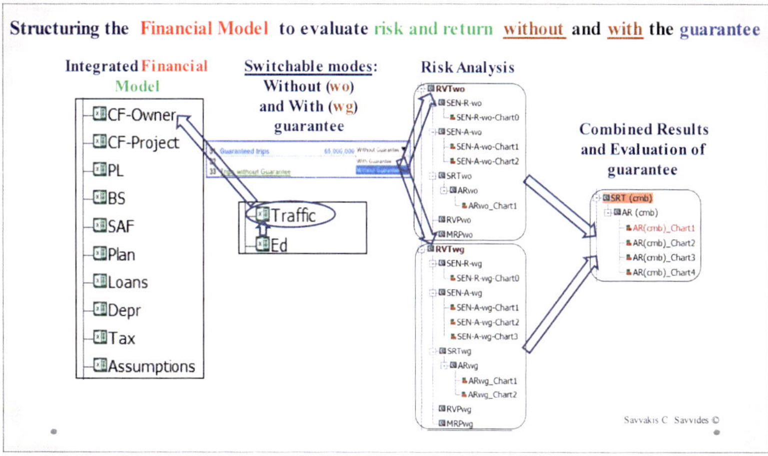

Method 1 – Setting Truncations for contracts to the inputs

By setting truncation limits to probability distributions defined as risk variables to a financial model prepared for Monte Carlo Simulation risk analysis it is possible to make two simulations as above where one is without the contract or guarantee in effect and a second one where the guarantee is presumed to be applied. In the latter case, the lower limits of the range in a probability distribution defined as input to the simulation such as for example the minimum number of trips attained, and which are covered by the concession party (usually a public authority) in the agreement are contained through applying a floor to the lower limit. The model is then simulated without the concession and again with the concession in place where the risk variable probability distributions essentially are cut off at the lower tail.

Figure 85 - Setting Truncations to limits during simulation

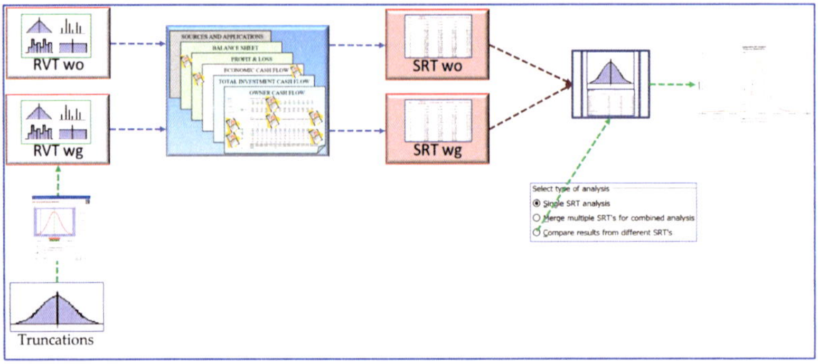

Method 2 – Modelling with and without guarantees for contracts in the outputs

Using a drop-down menu form and if statements in Excel sets up the affected cash flows to two states. One **without the guarantee** and one **with the guarantee. The financial model** runs in two modes where a trigger switches from one to the other. In the **With Guarantee** mode the assumptions about the guarantee set are allowed to affect the outcome. It is also possible to estimate the cost/price of the guarantee from the estimation of the annual payments that are thus calculated and stored in a Monte Carlo simulation process (Figure 71).

Figure 86 - Modelling the contract in the Outputs

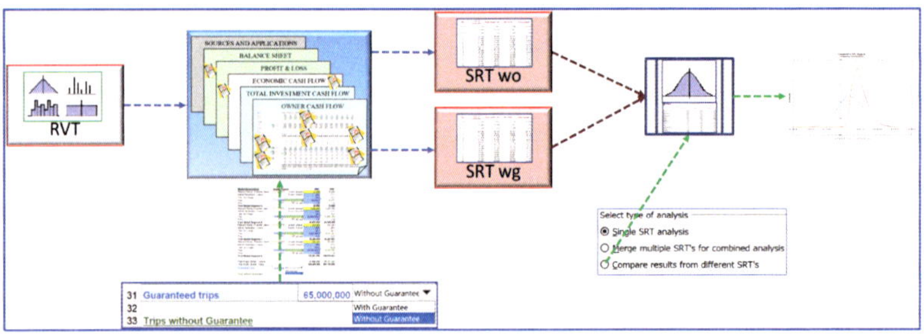

The Model is set and simulated in two modes and the results of the two simulations are then compared to extract the impact of a proposed guarantee on the various stakeholders (such as the Government and the Operator).

Figure 87 - Workbook Map for Motorway -With(wg)/Without(wo) Guarantee[68]

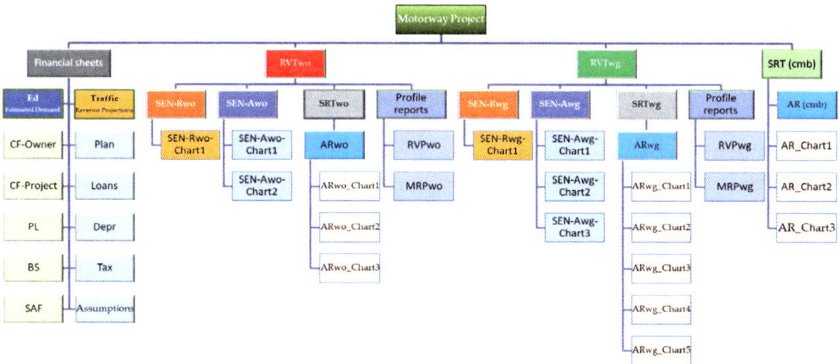

Figure 71 presents the structure of the modelling and simulation as applied. The trigger of the "with and without the guarantee" mode is in the Sheet Traffic. In the first instance the setting is put on the Without the Guarantee mode (in Risk Variables Table -RVTwo) as illustrated above. The Sensitivity is run and the Simulation stored in Table SRTwo for 5,000 scenarios in this mode. From that an Analysis of Results calculating all the relevant statistics stored in ARwo in Figure 87. From that, the risk/return profiles of the project under this assumption are extracted and presented in 3 charts (ARwo, 1, 2, and 3)

The exact same sequence and steps are then repeated but with the setting in sheet "Traffic" set to calculate and consider the proposed guarantee (RVTwg tree in Figure 71). Following that RiskEase allows the combining and comparing the results of the two modes. This is shown under in SRT(cmb).

The crop and some of the results of this process is demonstrated below.

The "With" and "Without" comparison

RiskEase enables the easy comparison of the results of two or more simulations. By comparing the output of With and Without Simulations one can extract and measure the shift in risk from one party to another because of the undertaking of a contractual obligation (Figure 72).

[68] *The Workbook Map was created following Monte Carlo simulation by using RiskEase© by RiskEase Ltd.*

Given that a private investor is not risk neutral (in other words the weights attached to the risk of losing are higher than the ones that one attaches for gaining the same amounts), how do we determine the shift of risk and return required to make the decision to invest for a Project Owner from negative to positive? How much of a shift is required and indeed justified to be in the public interest for the investment from the point of view of the Owner to become acceptable?

In the Motorway example the Project Owner's probability distribution of Net Present Value without and with the guarantee is displayed in Figure 88.

Figure 88 - The effect of the Concession on the Project Owner

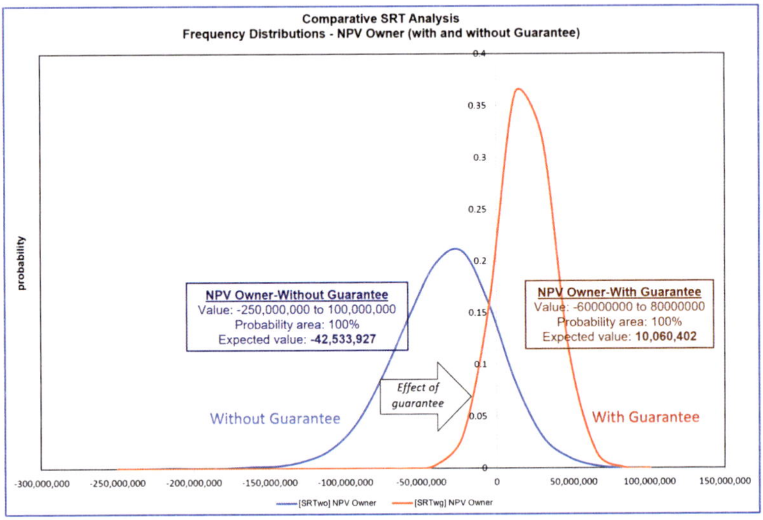

A contract benefit by one project party is a counter cost to another. An improvement in the NPV and risk profile of the project owner in a concession agreement between the Public Sector and a private investor should not make the private sector project owner indifferent to the inherent business risk. The benefit to be conceded to a private sector party should not in principle make the Owner risk profile overwhelmingly positive and practically devoid of business risk.

A contract benefit by one project party is a counter cost to another. An improvement in the NPV and risk profile of the project owner in a concession agreement between the Public Sector and a private investor will cause a corresponding deterioration in the Economy's NPV and Risk

Profile. The benefit to be conceded to a private sector party, if taken as a cost to the economy rather than a mere transfer, should not make the Economy's NPV and risk profile negative or too risky.

General rules for entering contracting concessions in PPPs

1. A project should be **economically viable** in the first place.
2. Contract undertakings in project finance should aim to create situations of **non zero-sum benefits**. The project owner should have an incentive to maximise return and deal with inherent business risks.
3. The benefit to be conceded to a private sector party should **not outweigh the economic benefits with excessive costs and inherent risks for the taxpayer**.
4. Unfortunately, often in PPP agreements such undertakings are put together without considering the above and are merely a method for **privatising the benefits and socialising the costs**.

Economic Analysis considerations:

5. As a rule, the benefit to be conceded to a private sector party should **not make the Economy's NPV and risk profile negative** or **too risky**.
6. However, the **third postulate of welfare Economics** assumes this possibility away. Any price paid by a public sector entity in a private sector partnership with a local stakeholder is assumed to be **an internal transfer** and therefore cannot, by definition, affect the economic cash flows of such projects.
7. This third postulate is however a rather **"heroic" assumption as regards PPP contracts.** While it is recognised that it is a fundamental assumption at the very **foundations of the methodology** and practice of economic analysis in project appraisal. One should not responsibly consider the transfer of a concession from a Public Authority to a private sector as a mere transfer that has no cost to the public at large.
8. Redistribution of wealth does affect economic welfare and there are many instances in the world that this is proven to be the case. Deals done under the veil of this broad assumption inevitably lead to **crony capitalism** with the private sector party being granted a red carpet to **extract rents**.

The impact of the guarantee should be to enable the financing of an economically viable project but not to socialise the risk emanating from it. The contract offered between stakeholders in a PPP capital investment project should go no further than making the financing of an economically viable project possible

In the motorway case example, the guarantee enables the project owner to also raise the debt financing needed. Without the guarantee the debt service coverage was below what would be considered an acceptable repayment capability by a financing institution. The effect of the guarantee, particularly in the initial years however make the debt financing acceptable and therefore possible. How contracts change the profile and shift risk among stakeholders. A contract shifts risk and can change the loan repayment profile of the project.

Figure 89 - Impact of Guarantee on debt financing

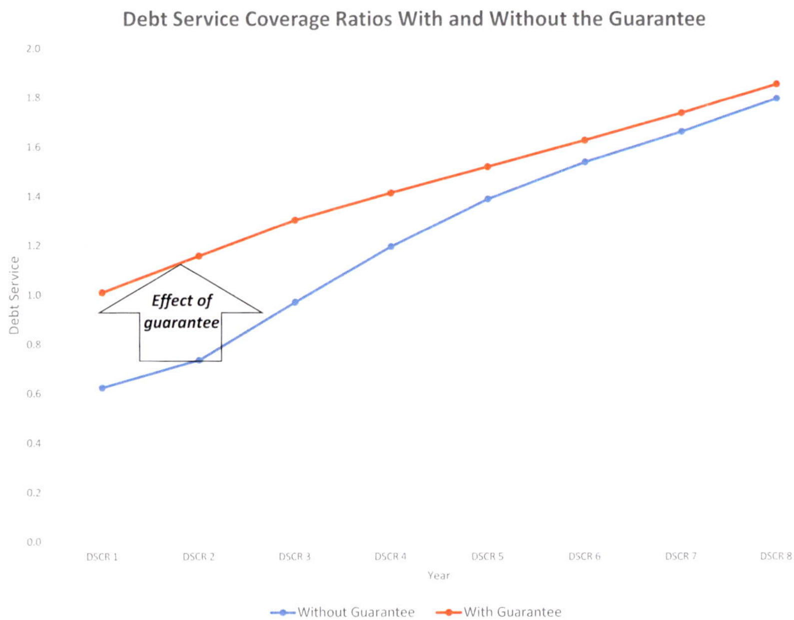

Need for proper evaluation and assessment of concessions

How to contain crony deals between the private and public sector

- *Without* proper **public sector comparator** studies and **independent economic analysis** and under the veil of promoting economic development **dubious agreements** between the public and the private sector are adopted and implemented.
- These contracts, often, result in **passing the business risk to the public sector** and lead to **Government created monopolies**.
- Such agreements merely achieve to **privatise the gains** of risky investment projects and to **socialise the costs**.
- The problem is not that the private sector, as expected, is always looking for loopholes to exploit and take advantage of. What is needed is for the public sector to independently study and meticulously evaluate the return and risks from such agreements before agreeing on a concession.

Economic analysis for public sector projects

Economic analysis is conducted on the premise that internal transfers between economic agents within the country (whereby one loses and another gains) ***cancel out*** and these are therefore not considered to be adding or subtracting anything from the net result as far as the national economy is concerned. In other words, the net present value of a capital investment project remains unaffected. This is indeed a heroic assumption which has the obvious benefit that it enables the calculation of the economic return of a capital investment project without worrying about exchanges within the national economy. To some extent this is supported by neo-classical economic thinking whereby it is presumed that the market sooner or later will iron out the wrinkles and by the survival of the fittest in a free market the overall economy becomes more efficient and will not turn out to be any worse off.

The third postulate of Welfare Economics

The third postulate of welfare Economics assumes this possibility away. Any price paid by a public sector entity in a private sector partnership with a local stakeholder is taken to be an internal transfer and therefore is an internal transfer and therefore, by definition of the third postulate of Welfare Economics, is taken as not affecting the economic cash flows or even the risk profile of such projects.

It is contended that the rules for entering contracting undertakings for public sector projects and Public Private Partnerships (PPPs) should not be governed by the rather naïve and over-simplified assumption that concessions in such projects from the public to private investors would optimise and cancel out. They do matter in more ways than one. These amounts are usually very substantial. Moreover, it is not a given that the market will optimise the benefits and costs among the economic agents and the population at large. But the biggest objection perhaps is the fact that the taxpayer in such circumstances is actually *bribing* private investors to undertake projects that they would not undertake without the concessions granted. In such mega projects the taxpayer ends up subsidizing the private sector stakeholders by grants and concessions that create monopolies and cartels. These are often extracting rents and cannot be considered as mere transfers that the market somehow irons out.

As a rule, therefore, it is proposed that in such capital investment projects the benefit to be conceded to a private sector party (through a grant or other concession) should *not make the Economy's NPV and the risk profile negative or too risky*. The concession should therefore be added to the cash flow as a cost and allowed to have an impact on the net cash flow and economic Net Present Value of the project.

It is recognised that the third postulate is a fundamental assumption at the very foundations of the methodology and practice of economic analysis in project appraisal. However, it must be pointed out that in other schools of economic thought the redistribution of wealth <u>does</u> affect economic welfare and there are many instances in the world that this is proven to be the case. Very often, deals done under the veil of this broad assumption for self-equilibrating markets inevitably lead to crony capitalism with the private sector party being granted a red carpet to extract rents. This is particularly so in major infrastructure projects which end up becoming Government created monopolies and cartels being handed over to private interests. In such circumstances, even under neo-classical thinking one cannot justify that such concessions by the public sector is justified as *monopolies* cannot be assumed to be optimising economic resources, nor maximising consumer surplus.

An example of the suggested methodology for evaluating guarantees in a motorway project is illustrated in the example below whereby a proposed guarantee is to be offered to the private sector vendors and managers of the new road. Through this example, a methodology is proposed on how to evaluate a guarantee. It also demonstrates how such decisions affect return for parties involved and how it may shift the risk from one stakeholder to another (usually the taxpayer).

References

1. Andreou Andreas, Jenkins Glenn, Savvides Savvakis C. 1990, *Tourism, Environment, and Profitability: The case of the Paphos Holiday Complex*, a case study in investment appraisal, HIID case study series, HIID Development Discussion paper No. 330, Harvard University, March 1990.
2. Andreou Andreas, Jenkins Glenn, Savvides Savvakis C. 1991, *Market competitiveness, Economic return and Risk: The case of the Limassol Juice Company*, a case study in investment appraisal, HIID case study series, HIID Development Discussion paper No. 380, Harvard University, July 1991.Assets of the hedge funds Worldwide (2020), Assets managed by hedge funds globally 2020, Statista, https://www.statista.com/statistics/271771/assets-of-the-hedge-funds-worldwide/
3. Assets of the hedge funds Worldwide (2020), Assets managed by hedge funds globally 2020, Statista, https://www.statista.com/statistics/271771/assets-of-the-hedge-funds-worldwide/
4. Black, William (2005) "The Best Way to Rob a Bank Is to Own One", University of Texas Press.
5. Bierman H. and Schmidt S. (1971), "The Capital Budgeting Decision" (McMillan Press, third edition).
6. Brealy R. and Myers S. (1991), "Principles of Corporate Finance" (McGraw Hill, fourth edition).
7. Bosch-Domenech Antoni and Silvestre Joaquim (2005), "Do the Wealthy Risk More Money? An Experimental Comparison", Universitat Pompeu Fabra and University of California, Davis
8. Carroll, Lewis (1872), "*Alice Through the Looking-Glass", Through the Looking-Glass, by Lewis Carroll. Illustrated by John Tenniel*
9. Day G. and Shocker A. and Srivastava R., "Customer-Oriented Approaches to identifying Product-Markets", Journal of Marketing, Fall 1979, pp.8-19.
10. Fisher, Irving (1933) "The debt-deflation theory of great depressions", Econometrica, Vol. 1, No.4
11. Gerhard Pohl and Dubravko Mihaljek, "Project Evaluation and Uncertainty in Practice: A Statistical Analysis of Rate-of-Return Divergences of 1,015 World Bank Projects" The World Bank

Economic Review, Volume 6, Number 2, pages 255-277, May 1992.
12. Glenday Graham (1989), Monte-Carlo Simulation Techniques in the Valuation of Truncated Distributions in the Context of Project Appraisal (Harvard Institute for International Development).
13. Glenday Graham (1998), "Risk-Sharing Contracts in Project Appraisal", Canadian Journal of Program Evaluation Special Issue 1998, Vol. 12, No. 3, pp. 99-120, https://www.utpjournals.press/doi/abs/10.3138/cjpe.
14. Harberger, Arnold (1987) "Reflections on Social Project Evaluation" in G. M. Meier (ed) Pioneers in Development, Vol. II, the World Bank and Oxford: Oxford University Press
15. Harberger, Arnold and Jenkins Glenn (2000) Manual for Cost Benefit Analysis of Investment Decisions, Cambridge, Massachusetts: Harvard Institute for International Development, 2000.
16. Harberger, Arnold (1971) "Three basic postulates for applied welfare economics," Journal of Economic Literature IX, No. 3, September: pp. 785-797
17. Hawkins C. J. and Pearce D. W. (1971), "Capital Investment Appraisal" (MacMillan Press).
18. Hertz David B. (1979), "Risk Analysis in Capital Investment", Harvard Business Review, 57(5), September-October.
19. Hertz David B. and Howard Thomas (1983), "Risk Analysis and its Applications" (John Wiley and sons).
20. Hertz David B. and Howard Thomas (1984), "Practical Risk Analysis" (John Wiley and sons).
21. Hudson, Michael (2012) Finance Capitalism and its discontents. ISLET-Verlag.
22. Hudson, Michael (2018) "'Creating Wealth' Through Debt: the West's Finance-Capitalist Road", May, https://www.counterpunch.org/2018/05/04/creating-wealth-through-debt-the-wests-finance-capitalist-road/
23. Jenkins, Glenn P. and Harberger Arnold C., "Cost-Benefit Analysis of Investment Decisions" Harvard Institute for International Development, 1991.
24. Jenkins, Glenn P., 1998. Evaluation of Stakeholder Impacts in Cost-Benefit Analysis, Harvard Institute *for International Development, Development Discussion Paper No. 631,1998.*
25. Jesse, Norman (2018), "Adam Smith, what he thought and why it matters", Penguin Allen Lane 2018.
26. Kavvadia Helen and Savvides Savvakis (2019) "Funding Economic Development and the Role of National Development Banks-The Case

of Cyprus", World Economics Journal, Vol. 21, No. 3, July–September
27. Koo, Richard (2015) The Escape from Balance Sheet Recession and the Q.E. Trap, Wiley.
28. Lessard Donald R (1988), "Risk-bearing and the choice of contract forms for oil exploration and Development", The Energy Journal, 5(1).
29. Levitt, Theodore, "Marketing Myopia" Harvard Business Review, Volume 53, Number 5, 1960.
30. Levy H. and Sarnat M. (1978), "Capital Investment and Financial Decisions" (Prentice-Hall).
31. Manison, Leslie and Savvides, Savvakis (2017) "Neglect private debt at the economy's peril", World Economics Journal, Vol. 18, No. 1, January–March.
32. Markowitz, Harry M. (1999). "The early history of portfolio theory: 1600–1960". Financial Analysts Journal. 55 (4): 5–16. doi:10.2469/faj.v55.n4.2281.
33. McBurnie Tony and Clutterbuck David, "The Marketing Edge" Penguin, 1988.
34. Mian, Atif (2014) House of Debt: How They (and You) Caused the Great Recession, and How We Can Prevent It from Happening Again, University of Chicago Press.
35. Minsky, Hyman (1992) "The Financial Instability Hypothesis", Levy Economics Institute of Bard College, Working Paper No. 74, May
36. Moran, William R., "Why New Products Fail", Journal of Advertising Research, April 1973, pp. 5-13.
37. Porterfield James T.S. (1965), "Investment Decisions and Capital Costs" (Prentice-Hall).
38. Pouliquen Louis Y. (1970), "Risk Analysis in Project Appraisal" World Bank Staff Occasional Papers no.11 (The John Hopkins University Press).
39. Reutlinger Shlomo (1970), "Techniques for Project Appraisal under Uncertainty", World Bank Staff Occasional Papers no. 10 (The John Hopkins University Press).
40. Paravisini Daniel, Rappoport Veronica, Ravina Enrichetta (2015), Risk Aversion and Wealth: Evidence from Person-to-Person Lending Portfolios, LSE and Columbia Discussion paper
41. RiskEase© Monte Carlo Simulation software by RiskEase Ltd, www.riskease.com.
42. Savvides, Savvakis C. *Risk Analysis in Investment Appraisal*, Project Appraisal Journal, Vol. 9, *No. 1,* pages 3-18, *March 1994.* Beech Tree Publishing. Republished in the book: *Cost–Benefit Analysis for Investment Decisions* (The International Library of Critical Writings in

Economics series, 152) by Arnold C. Harberger (Editor) and Glenn P. Jenkins (Editor) and Kuo Chum-Yan Kuo, by Edward Elgar Publishing (December 29, 2018)

43. Savvides, Savvakis C. *Market Analysis and Competitiveness in Project Appraisal, Harvard* Institute for International Development, Development Discussion Paper No. 755, February 2000.
44. Savvides, Savvakis C. *Corporate Lending and the Assessment of Credit Risk*, Journal of Money, Investment and Banking, Issue 20, March 2011.
45. Savvides, Savvakis (2012) *"Financial markets, bloated governments and the misallocation of capital"*, Journal of Finance and Investment Analysis, Vol. 1, No. 2: pp. 201-219.
46. Savvides, Savvakis (2014) *"The pursuit of economic development"*, Journal of Finance and Investment Analysis, Scienpress, Vol. 3, No. 2
47. Savvides, Savvakis C., (2022a) *"The disconnect of funding from wealth creation"*. World Economics Journal, Vol. 23, No. 2, June 2022.
48. Savvides, Savvakis C. (2022b), *"Risk Through the Looking Glass – The Pursuit of a Return Without the Risk"*. World Economics Journal, Vol. 23, No. 4, December 2022.
49. Savvides, Savvakis C. (2024), *"The Marketing Evaluation of Capital Investment Projects"*, World Economics, Vol. 25, No. 1, January–March 2024
50. Schnedler David E., "Use Strategic Market Models to Predict Customer Behaviour", Sloan Management Review, Spring 1996, Volume 37, Number 3, pp. 85-92.
51. Sharpe, William F. (1964). "Capital asset prices: A theory of market equilibrium under conditions of risk". Journal of Finance. 19 (3): 425–442.
52. Smith, Adam (2008) An Inquiry into the Nature and Causes of the Wealth of Nations: A Selected Edition, Edited by Kathryn Sutherland, Oxford Paperbacks
53. Vague, Richard (2014) The Next Economic Crisis: Why It's Coming and How to Avoid It, University of Pennsylvania Press.

APPENDIX

RiskEase© Monte Carlo Simulation software

RiskEase Ltd is a company specialising in producing software and providing training in capital investment appraisal and project finance. The *professional software* by RiskEase Ltd are essential tools that are constantly being adapted and improved by the company. But they are only one piece of what we call a *total package* which also includes *training* and *expert on-the-job advice*. This is why we do not define our business as being in software development alone. This is not by chance but rather by design. It is also what differentiates us from other vendors of similar but general-purpose Monte Carlo simulation software. Our software applications are designed and developed to best serve the needs of decision makers in capital investments, corporate lending and project finance. What enables us to walk this path successfully and continually improve our software is that we are also practitioners having one foot firmly on the field of investment appraisal and project finance.

The RiskEase Design

At the heart of our competitive edge over other similar software lies the core and superior design of RiskEase which enables the user to go beyond the constraints usually being imposed by such applications. The original software was called RiskMaster and was released in 1986 as a Lotus 1-2-3 add-on[69]. The basic design since then has been enhanced and improved a great deal. However, the underlying concept remained in place. The idea was to enable a professional analyst involved in the appraisal and assessment of risk in a capital investment project to link the risk variables (the most uncertain and sensitive inputs) of a financial model and the formulas that are of interest in the measurement of return and risk (such the Net Present Value, the Internal Rate of Return or even the year-by-year Debt Service Coverage ratios of a loan and so on).

By design, RiskEase does not change the user financial model. One is simply enabled very easily to provide the links to it necessary to run the simulation (and do the Sensitivity Analysis). There is no need therefore to keep different versions of the user financial model. Another key and by design difference is that the Probability distributions are not provided by mystic names that may make sense only to scientists or research practitioners. They are presented in 5 families of probability types which however can with great easy be adapted to approximate any other pre-defined probability distribution. There are three symmetrical types (Uninform/trapezoidal, Triangular and Normal). These can all be visually skewed, shifted or truncated to take practically any pattern that the user expects a particular risk variable to conform to. Similarly, there are two Custom Probability Distribution types (Step and Discrete). The user is enabled with great easy to define intervals and nodes respectively and attach probability weights. There is also a supplementary library of specific Probability Distributions and the ability to save new patterns created by the user. It is also possible to create a Probability Distribution to user provided data. RiskEase reads the data and applies a goodness alternating and finding the best settings from the five family types of Probability Distributions provided.

[69] RiskMaster for DOS was in fact one of the very first applications to work on a financial model spreadsheet directly. This and its successor software (RiskMaster for Windows and RiskEase version 1.x both Excel Add-ins) were used routinely on the Program in Investment Appraisal and Management at Harvard University were Savvakis Savvides was a regular visiting lecturer).

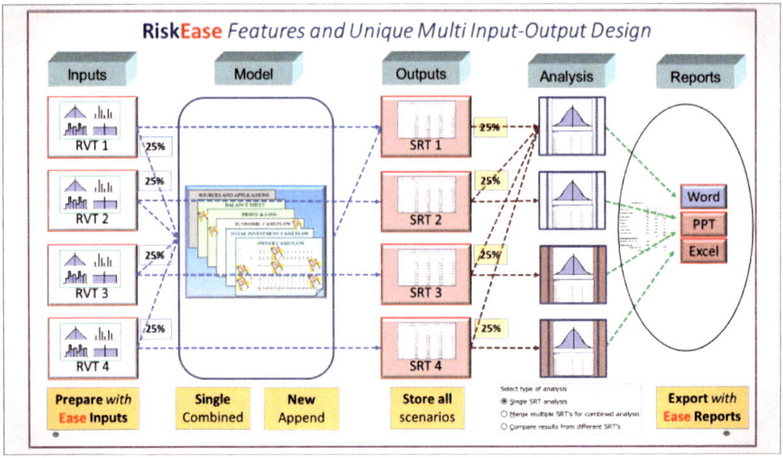

Another unique feature of the RiskEase design is that it allows multiple inputs and outputs. The user assumptions (links, Inputs-Risk Variables defined and Formulas-Model Results and any correlations) are defined in a special template called the Risk Variables Table (RVT). It is thus possible to define any number of RVTs and even to combine them with weights in a simulation. Hence, a simulation creates a Simulation Runs Table (SRT) which is also accessible with all the scenarios in it to the user to scrutinise. This can be created or if another SRT exists, to be appended on. It can also be created as mentioned above by combining the inputs from several RVTs.

The same multi-input-output logic holds true when several SRTs are created. These can be analysed on their own or in combination. The Analyse Results module can also Merge and Compare the results from several simulations (putting together a number of SRTs).

The "Analyse Results" module can create a table from a host of available user-selected statistics. It is also equipped with a very powerful Charting which enables one to analyse in-depth the wisdom that is contained in the Simulation data. Over and above the usual Frequency and Cumulative probability distributions produced by all such software, RiskEase has a set of additional analysis that the user can undertake through special charting capabilities. Such the Confidence Range plot which can plot a series of model results and show where these could deviate to at pre-set standard deviations from the mean. It also includes a Segmentation Analysis capability (for both Frequency and Cumulative Probability Distributions) which enable the sophisticated user to extract and present the essence of risk from the simulations. One can therefore dissect and estimate at the click of a button the Expected Value, Expected Loss, and Expected Gain of a probability distribution emerging form a simulation. It also shows the area and the probability of segments in the tails of the probability distribution reviewed. And it creates Excel charts which one can use easily in a report.

The Report module is also designed no compromises on functionality but with ease of use for providing the data one needs to include in a professional report. It creates a Risk Variables Profile and Model Results Profile which clearly and graphically present the assumptions used in the simulation. Furthermore, the Custom Report module enables one to select all outputs of a simulation process and export at the click of a button to Word, PowerPoint, and Excel.

RiskEase is a complete state-of-the-art software product which evolves and changes according to the needs of professional on the field of credit risk assessment and project finance. Its purpose is to enhance the competence of such professional with the utmost ease.

INDEX